I Apologize

...but not like you think

Jim McCracken

I Apologize ...but not like you think
Copyright © 2024 Jim McCracken
All rights reserved.

Print Edition
ISBN: 978-1-7335713-2-6
Published by Jim McCracken, 2024

No parts of this publication may be reproduced, stored in a retrieval system, or transmitted in any form or by any means, electronic, mechanical, photocopying, recording, or otherwise, without the prior written permission of the copyright owner.

This book is sold subject to the condition that it shall not, by way of trade or otherwise, be lent, resold, hired out, or otherwise circulated without the publisher's prior consent in any form of binding or cover other than that in which it is published and without a similar condition including this condition being imposed on the subsequent purchaser. Under no circumstances may any part of this book be photocopied for resale.

Scripture taken from the NEW AMERICAN STANDARD BIBLE,
Copyright © 1960, 1962, 1963 1968, 1971, 1972,
1973 1975, 1977, 1995 by The Lockman Foundation
All rights reserved
Used by permission.
http://www.Lockman.org

Cover design by Jim McCracken and Emma Scheaffer
Interior design by Jim McCracken and Emma Scheaffer
Cover images are stock photos by permission

DEDICATIONS

To... Deb, my one life partner "under the sun," faithful wife who excels them all, editor-in-chief, fellow adventurer to the end... and beyond....

For... our three daughters (Ellie, Sarah, & Kate), their chosen men, twelve grandchildren (Nelson, Audrey, Allison, Adelaide, Samuel, North, Selah, Katherine, Hazel, Shiloh, Norah, & Lucy), and the generations to come with the hope of helping them survive and overcome this insane world in which they live

Thanks to... Emma Scheaffer who lent her skills to wrap up this package in pleasing digital and pulp modalities (typesetting and cover design of Kindle and paperback versions)

CONTENTS

SECTION A
SKETCHY IDEAS ABOUT WHO'S WHO & WHAT'S WHAT

#1   Every generation thinks its era was the golden one. That's just nostalgia. They're all basically the same.

#2   Look how far man has progressed! People aren't stupid. Humanism is supreme.

#3   We need to save the planet. And I'm not sure animals should be eaten by humans either.

#4   People are basically good. It's the imposed traditional social constructs that mess them up.

#5   Multiculturalism is positive and desirable. Cross-cultural exposure and interaction bring advancement.

#6   Pride is not a sin. One should rightly be proud of himself, his work, his accomplishments… just not unduly prideful.

SECTION B
WISHING IT'S SUCH DOESN'T MAKE IT SO

#7   You think your beliefs are right just like everybody else thinks theirs are. Everyone has only his own opinion and interpretation.

#8   This life is all there is. There is nothing after this.

#9   Evolution (macroevolution) is scientific fact.

#10   Good will win out over bad. There's a reason for whatever happens (a disappointment, delay, tragedy).

#11   Stop thinking binary! Everything is multi-faceted, possibilities endless, interpretations individualized. There are no absolutes.

#12   Dystopias are just fiction, as are utopias.

#13   I'm not like most people. I'm different, kind of odd, even strange. I do my own thing.

SECTION C
KNEE-JERK ATTACKS ON TRADITIONAL VALUES

#14   You're racist. You're prejudiced. Are you prejudiced?

#15   Abortion—a woman has a right to her own body. It's ultimately her call.

#16   Unlimited gender types, gender neutral, gender fluid, intersex—they're all valid. You're homophobic. You're transphobic.

#17   Equality is the goal and equity is the means of accomplishing it. [applied to gender, race, handicaps, opportunity, socio-economics, etc.]

SECTION D
JUST PLAIN SILLY SEMI-RELIGIOUS NOTIONS

#18   You have to love yourself before you can love others.

#19   Loving all is the goal. You're not loving, but a hater because you don't accept _____.

#20 I believe that the Universe knows, controls, and determines all.

#21 You can't understand what I'm going through because you've never _____." [been gay, lost a child, struggled with addiction, been poor, etc.]

#22 My faith, my Christianity, is a personal thing.

#23 If you believe enough, you can do anything. You just have to have faith.

SECTION E
POPULAR BUT WRONG IDEAS ABOUT CHRISTIANITY

#24 The Christian message is so negative and pessimistic. Sin, repenting, lost people, hell... really?

#25 It's the exclusivity of Christianity with which I disagree. Religion should be inclusive. Besides, all religions are basically the same and have the same goals at heart.

#26 Why can't Christians accept others' beliefs also and just get along with those who believe differently?

#27 You're not to judge others. You can't know what's in people's hearts.

#28 Christians believe money is the root of all evils. That's a bit extreme!

SECTION F
CONFUSION ABOUT THE CHURCH

#29 The church should be seeker friendly, welcoming and accepting of all kinds of people.

#30 The church will prevail regardless. God says so. *I will build My church and the gates of Hades will not overpower it.* (Mt. 16:18)

#31 Doctrinal statements are essential for churches, denominations, para-church organizations.

#32 The church is here to change the world. It should fight evil and promote good. [mainly promulgated by believers as "bringing in the Kingdom"]

#33 Women in the church are way behind those outside. They're still second-class citizens, doormats, suppressed.

SECTION G
SKEWED IDEAS CHRISTIANS SOMETIMES HOLD

#34 Why do Christians blindly support Israel? The Jews killed Jesus!

#35 Missionaries are special Christians—either super spiritual or a little weird and can't fit in their own culture.

#36 Ecclesiastes is depressing. Solomon was a mess.

#37 Do you think that person is saved?

#38 I just speak my mind to God—raw, honest, about everything, whatever... even complaining like David did. God can handle it. Jacob wrestled with God!

#39 Information technology advancement, Artificial Intelligence in particular, is inevitable. Christians just need to be aware and careful.

#40 A Christian should take care of his body as the temple of the Holy Spirit.

#41 One emphasizes, "Christians shouldn't be lazy."
Another says, "Christians shouldn't strive."
Which is it?

#42 The Bible is so hard to understand. I can't really quote
verses word-for-word and remember exactly where
things are in Scripture.

#43 Have you read so-and-so's Christian book, _____?

#44 Christians should be positive people, not negative
people. Positivity is Christian.

#45 Christians have 2nd Amendment rights also. And it makes
sense for a church to protect its families with armed
security or congregants "packing".

#46 Our pets are part of the family. They'll be in heaven, won't
they? What about the lion lying down with
the lamb verse?

#47 Christians have complete freedom to pursue any
career, barring outright sinful activity.

SECTION H
SEEING BUT NOT BELIEVING

#48 How do you explain so-called "evil people" and those of
other religions thriving or living to old age?

#49 This world is insane!

#50 Most people need therapy at some time. Modern
culture creates so much stress.

#51 What's with this current generation of young people?
They're so messed up and lost.

SECTION I
EXCUSES FOR NOT BELIEVING

#52 **I'm not antagonistic toward Christianity. I just don't see the evidence.**

#53 **The church is full of hypocrites. I'm not a Christian because of all the hypocrites.**

#54 **He's so heavenly minded he's of no earthly good.**

#55 **What kind of god allows evil and then would kill his own son to fix the mess?**

#56 **I've met lots of religious people and they sure haven't made me want to be one of them.**

#57 **Christianity is a bunch of "Thou Shalt Nots". What's the appeal of avoiding all the fun and exciting things in this life? And a god who demands that to let you into heaven? No thanks!**

SECTION J
AND ONE TO GROW ON

∞ **Who needs religion? What's the big deal? I can find my own way or make my own path.**

WHAT IS THIS BOOK?

Why do the nations rage and the peoples plot in vain?

This book reflects my personal attempt to stand firm—to keep my feet amidst the flailing culture in which I live. If others reading this are aided in their stand against the empty insanity, I consider it a victory.

In seeing this book's title, you may have thought that I am apologizing in today's oh-so-popular style that claims to somehow take responsibility for past generations' failures or sins (slavery, LGBTQ+ insensitivity, carbon emissions, being white, being male, being human, etc.). I am not. Although I am sympathetic to some of the justifiable complaints, I have very little hope that those knee-jerk apologies will have any real or positive effects. Apologies are appropriate responses when real offenses have taken place, genuine repentance inspires the offender, and potentially restorative actions are sensible; but that's not what I observe to be the popular version today. And I don't believe it's what those calling for apologies really want. They typically demonstrate a core motive more akin to revenge, tit-for-tat, self-exoneration, or self-serving agendas. When "reparations" typically take the form of punch-drunk monetary proposals or overreaching legislative demands... I'm beyond suspicious. I'm incredulous. I won't lie down or take a fall. So, no, I am not apologizing thusly.

Another less popular and more erudite form of apology is that of religious, and specifically Christian, defense of doctrines through systematic argumentation or discourse. You may have thought that that is what I am attempting here. Well, yes and no. Yes, as to the purpose of defending the faith against those who don't understand or agree with God's Word. But no, as to the systematic and thorough treatment of doctrines. That has been and is being done by the likes of more capable men like G. K. Chesterton, C. S. Lewis, John Lennox, and William Lane Craig. Apologists such as these outstrip my research and organizational capacities, much more my core intellect. Ligonier Ministries alone has a regular line-up of apologists more thoroughly equipped than I am. Those warriors reach an audience willing to fight through the arguments in debate halls or lengthy written treatments. My hat is off to those who have the ability and inclination to make a lifework of thorough, formal apologetics. I am not a heavyweight. So, I am not exactly apologizing like that either.

This apology has the same purpose at heart as the latter category above, but in bite-size, random-fashion blurbs provoked by current events and trends. These short retorts were written off-the-cuff in response to daily observations made over several years and stuffed in my phone notes. However, though off-the-cuff, the responses were not merely reactionary rants or ill-considered conclusions. Theological training and ministry experience have afforded me opportunity to be deeply engrossed in study and meditation on Christian truth up against culture for five decades now. I have crafted these simple apologetic briefs for the common man (most specifically, my progeny of children, children's children, and so forth...) with the not-so-lofty hope of **prompting some pause for thought**. Maybe an abrupt, poignant jab in the midst of our pop culture's shouting match will jar to awakeness (as opposed to wokeness) those who have gotten woozy, are staggering and about to drop. The topics are not contrived or rare. I come across them every day. My apologies don't try to argue from every possible facet or with layers of substantiating support, although that is patently available and has certainly fed into what is written here. They are also not just off-the-huff tirades with vitriol for those who believe differently. To borrow the overworked phrase—it's not personal.

These apologetic one-two punches are directed at the wild swings of our pugilistic culture that increasingly rages against all sanity... and ultimately against the God that gave it breath and legs on which to stand.

Why do the nations rage and the peoples plot in vain?

Finally, be strong in the Lord and in the strength of His might. Put on the full armor of God, so that you will be able to stand firm against the schemes of the devil. For our struggle is not against flesh and blood, but against the rulers, against the powers, against the world forces of this darkness, against the spiritual forces of wickedness in the heavenly *places. Therefore, take up the full armor of God, so that you will be able to resist in the evil day, and having done everything, to stand firm. Stand firm therefore...*

There Is A Line
Written by Wayne Kirkpatrick & Billy Sprague
Recorded by Susan Ashton

It's hard to tell just when the night becomes the day
That golden moment when the darkness rolls away
But there is a moment none the less
In the regions of the heart there is a place
A sacred charter that should not be erased
It is the marrow, the moral core that I cannot ignore

Within the scheme of things
Well I know where I stand
My convictions they define who I am
Some move the boundaries at any cost
But there is a line I will not cross
No riding on the fence - no alibis
No building on the sands of compromise
I won't be borrowed and I can't be bought
No, there is a line I will not cross

Ask the ocean where the water meets the land
He will tell you it depends on where you stand
And you're neither right or wrong
But in the fathoms of the soul that won't ring true
'Cause truth is more than an imposing point of view
It rises above the changing tide as sure as the morning sky

Within the scheme of things
Well I know where I stand
My convictions they define who I am
Some move the boundaries at any cost
But there is a line I will not cross
No riding on the fence - no alibis
No building on the sands of compromise
I won't be borrowed and I can't be bought
No, there is a line I will not cross

SECTION A:

SKETCHY IDEAS ABOUT WHO'S WHO & WHAT'S WHAT

#1

When someone says...

Every generation thinks its era was the golden one. That's just nostalgia. They're all basically the same.

I apologize, but...

Agreed. The nature of mankind is basically the same, and nostalgia can taint and distort honest reflection. However, eras of history are certainly varied—sometimes wildly, dramatically—even in a relatively short period of time. To be quite recent and local, imagine a child growing up in bombed WWII Europe or under the despotic Idi Amin. Should he think that was "normal life", especially if it was compared to an average childhood in 1950s America? Do you really think a typical American childhood experience or work ethic in 1930s depression era is the same as that of a 1950s or 1980s youth? And that's just a 50-year span and one subculture of the world.

Imagine attempting to draw a comparison between an American high school student's life today with a similarly aged young man or woman in Middle Ages Saxony or 1000 BC Africa! Some places and some eras are extremely different from ours—better in some ways, worse in others. All times are not the same. To not know that as fact is to be enormously obtuse to history, trends, and today's manic social reactionism, as opposed to having informed, contextualized, and rational thoughtfulness.

Let me propose one simplistic observation among millions possible. Barbarism of ancient times had some legitimate excuse, due to sheer lack of knowledge and tangible advancement. Fast-forward thousands of years and cultures to the enlightenment and scientific ages, barbarism receded into fewer and smaller pockets. Such things as the adoption of a common civility, accepted Judeo-Christian morals, sanitation, healthcare, and a Protestant work ethic were real, observable, historical manifestations—far from perfect, but observable progress from savagery!

Now, proceed a few more revolutions to the current times of our "advanced" America. Instead of a greater level of peace like the 1960s naively hallucinated, a new barbarism has emerged. In place of an anticipated nationally increasing educational level, and a caring, fair, tolerant society, a revisited Dark Ages is popularized, in which meanness, sexual perversion, mental illness, and senseless violence pervade our daily news; but this time, the barbarism is volitional and self-imposed. *But realize this, that **in the last days** difficult time will come. For people will be lovers of self, lovers of money, boastful, arrogant, slanderers, disobedient to parents, ungrateful, unholy, unloving, irreconcilable, malicious gossips, without self-control, brutal, haters of good, treacherous, reckless, conceited, lovers of pleasure rather than lovers of God, holding to a form of godliness, although they have denied its power... always learning and never coming to a knowledge of the truth.* (2 Tim. 3:1-7) That sounds more like the successful line-up for a blockbuster evening of current television, instead of the prescient warning it was written to be!

Time does advance. People and the cultures they create do not always.

No wonder some of us find a little unrealistic comfort in nostalgia.

I Apologize ...but not like you think

#2

When someone says...

Look how far man has progressed! People aren't stupid. Humanism is supreme.

I apologize, but...

Man **is** amazing! But no intelligent person would marvel at a modern computer and praise its capabilities without having the names Bill Gates and Steve Jobs subconsciously tucked in their brain right behind that conscious thought. That's appropriate. And yet most people look at mankind and ascribe "first cause" attributes to him... without any thought of the awesome Designer-God behind man's genius, not to mention his existence. Man may be the pinnacle of *creation*, but that reality should prompt a thinking person to drop to the ground in adoration of One who could actually speak man into existence! However, in staggering contrast, the overwhelming preponderance of mankind ignore Him completely or design a god of their own conceptions. This is nothing new to Christian knowledge. It's the natural result of man's original fall, his rebellious idolatry, and the reason why God's offer of forgiveness and relationship is so... truly amazing!

The history of people on earth clearly records some impressive genius among mankind. It also records a general meanness among the masses—ever-present murder and warring, starvation from selfish distribution of food, oppression of legitimate entities such as women, children, races, the disabled, to list just a few evidences.

Intelligent and wise men and women over the millennia have been motivated to make life work well and so contributed something for others to build upon. Today is a unique era in which unproven, unjudged information is universally disseminated. The glut of information fools the foolish masses into thinking that they are knowledgeable and wise. Anyone and everyone "puts it out there" for the world to pick-and-choose with reckless abandon. And those who want to have some influence rule the day with ignorance, despising and challenging the genuinely knowledgeable and wise ones. All it takes to gain or lose a following is a "like" or "dislike", and the mindless inertia begins to disseminate in terabytes per second! Those building upon the wisdom of the ages and voicing it are dismissed with sadly effective disparaging epithets, such as archaic, backwards, haters, something-phobic.

What to do?! The likes of one highly influential humanist, Stanley Kubric, offers this: "However vast the darkness, we must supply our own light." The God who created all the Stanleys of the world generously offers these perspectives: *God is light and in Him is no darkness at all.* (1 Jn. 1:5) *And God said, "Let there be light."* (Gen. 1:3) *Wisdom excels folly as light excels darkness.* (Eccl. 2:13) Two very different pictures. And the frames of reference are as different as… well… night and day!

I Apologize ...but not like you think

#3

When someone says...

We need to save the planet. And I'm not sure animals should be eaten by humans either.

I apologize, but...

Although it's wise to take care of the earth, the Christian knows and trusts a "deeper magic" that the unbeliever doesn't—that the earth will remain and survive and (spoiler alert!)... man doesn't destroy it! For starters, the Christian believes creation history in the Bible, which reveals that it was God who, looking at each stage of His handiwork from stars to starfish, declared that *it was good.* Then God makes mankind, stating *it was very good.* Next, some of the relationships of this world continue to be clarified for us. *God created man in His own image, in the image of God He created him; male and female He created them.* (Gen. 1:27) Notice the emphasis by repetition that mankind alone bears His image! *Be fruitful and multiply, and fill the earth, and subdue it; and rule over the fish of the sea and over every living thing that moves on the earth.* (Gen. 1:28) Humans filling the earth isn't the problem, but the plan. Over-population? No problem, God's got it. Man using natural resources, eating plants and animals? *Every moving thing that is alive shall be food for you; I give all to you, as I gave the green plant.* (Gen. 9:3) It's all here for mankind's sustenance and enjoyment.

Sketchy Ideas About Who's Who & What's What

But couldn't mankind destroy it through pollution and overuse? No, but he could possibly make it less pleasurable and more difficult to live in. His subduing it should be done with wisdom, as a good caretaker of His Creator's generosity; but he can't destroy it. *While the earth remains, seedtime and harvest, and cold and heat, and summer and winter, and day and night shall not cease.* (Gen. 8:22) Some answers to concerns about the earth's future are available to people, if they're willing to listen.

So, a final bit of even deeper magic that the Christian knows and trusts – how the earth **does** end! *But the Day of the Lord will come like a thief, in which the heavens will pass away with a roar and the elements will be destroyed with intense heat, and the earth and its works will be burned up.* (2 Pet. 3:10) Man doesn't slowly destroy it. What a relief! God does it when mankind doesn't expect it *(like a thief)*... in an instant. How is that good news? *Then I saw a new heaven and a new earth; for the first heaven and the first earth passed away...* (Rev. 21:1) *Behold, I am making all things new.* (Rev. 21:5) Whew... that is a relief. But for whom? *Things which eye has not seen and ear has not heard, and which have not entered the heart of man, all that God has prepared* *for those who love Him. For to us* God *has revealed them through the Spirit; for the Spirit searches all things, even the depths of God.* (1 Cor. 2:9-10)

There **is** that... the deeper magic. Do **you** believe the magic?

I Apologize ...but not like you think

#4

When someone says...

People are basically good. It's the imposed traditional social constructs that mess them up.

I apologize, but...

Both the conclusion and the premise are wrong. The whole together is unsubstantiated and nonsensical. Social constructs are made by people. So if the constructs are faulty, it's because people are faulty. Good doesn't produce bad, nor vice-versa. The fact is that every place and every era of history has been filled with war, violence, oppression, inequity, division, greed, pollution, deceitfulness, foolishness... all of which came from one common source—mankind and no other. To not own that truth is to be blinded to reality or willfully dishonest. The simultaneous fact that love and goodness exist in the world does offer us hope, but in no way suggests that man is its source or that he is innately good.

Examples: If I were to offer you a glass of water that was 67% pure, but 33% sewage, would you conclude the water is basically pure and drink it? 1 in 3 Americans have criminal records. 1 in 2 marriages can't stay together. Among collegians, 80-90% can no longer distinguish male and female. Almost 100% admit they lie.

Sketchy Ideas About Who's Who & What's What

If man was good, society would be good. It's just the opposite. Society's problems start within each man's depraved mind. *And just as they did not see fit to acknowledge God any longer, God gave them over to a depraved mind, to do those things which are not proper, being filled with all unrighteousness, wickedness, greed, evil; full of envy, murder, strife, deceit, malice; they are gossips, slanderers, haters of God, insolent, arrogant, boastful, inventors of evil, disobedient to parents, without understanding, untrustworthy, unloving, unmerciful.* (Rom. 1:28-31) And once each man is corrupted, instead of changing course, he doubles down and condones others' depravity, creating a corrupt society. *And although they know the ordinance of God, that those who practice such things are worthy of death, they not only do the same, but also give hearty approval to those who practice them.* (Rom. 1:32)

The wisest man ever, Solomon, studying and searching for hopeful meaning in every aspect of life concluded, *The hearts of the sons of men are full of evil and insanity is in their hearts throughout their lives.* (Eccl. 9:3) Today's "sons of men" fill university podiums with lectures of man's supposed inherent goodness and society's encroaching evil, and their student minions fill social media platforms repeating the irrational non-sequitur argument. That it is men who create societies and traditions is lost on them! These groundless professors and unfounded social media pundits are adrift. Unsurprisingly, Solomon's assessment appears spot on.

I Apologize ...but not like you think

#5

When someone says...

Multiculturalism is positive and desirable. Cross-cultural exposure and interaction bring advancement.

I apologize, but...

Maybe yes, maybe no. The **potential** for advancement, broadened exposure, enriching experience, and enhanced knowledge exists. (I have personally and consciously lived a life and career that pursued such possibilities.) And yet the reality is that cross-cultural exposure and interaction has every bit as much potential for decline and evil as for advancement and good. Certain quantities of melatonin, exotic language accents, interesting clothing styles, surprising music types, and new food menus offer **no** automatic promise for bettering one's life. They all depend on the character of the people in that culture and the foreigner interacting with it. A near-sighted man may turn right into an optometrist's office. Or that same man might turn left into a pickpocket's lair. Difference and change are neither automatically better nor worse. Both potentials are possible. It takes insight and applied wisdom to recognize both and interact fittingly. *A prudent man sees evil and hides himself, the naive proceed and pay the penalty.* (Prov. 27:12)

For the moment, geographic borders provide one smart hesitation to observe and discern!

#6

When someone says...

Pride is not a sin. One should rightly be proud of himself, his work, his accomplishments... just not unduly prideful.

I apologize, but...

Aaaah, "unduly" is a revealing word here. That's humanism (man-at-the-top) talking. It is ignorant and blind to the reality that God alone is at the top. And even He is not prideful, but humble in that uncontested place. Man is merely a creature, albeit gloriously and uniquely made in the image of his Creator. Still, that's an immeasurable difference!

No, pride is not a good thing. Not even a little pride. (Hey Christians... Dove Awards? Really?) In fact, pride was the first sin and is the progenitor of all sins. It is such because it distorts reality, which starts an unending chain of error and perversion. Pride started man's fall. Man is wholesale fallen and distorts all he touches. God, however, being totally Other (the core meaning of "Holy"), must be recognized as such in order for man to not wrongly view himself; that is, to not take pride in anything.

Every good thing given and every perfect gift is from above, coming down from the Father of lights. (Jas. 1:17) Therefore, God rightly *opposes the proud, but gives grace to the humble.* (Jas. 4:6)

To put it in simple statements:
- Pride is not fitting to man.
- Pride is not necessary or descriptive of God.

Pride is, in the truest sense of the word, vanity... vain, empty, nothing. The phrase "empty pride" is redundant. Pride is a fantasy, a name without a being, a descriptive without an object, a fairytale without a single character.

SECTION B:

WISHING IT'S SUCH DOESN'T MAKE IT SO

#7

When someone says...

You think your beliefs are right just like everybody else thinks theirs are. Everyone has only his own opinion and interpretation.

I apologize, but...

First off, I do not think **I'm** right. Like all children growing up, I was immature and typically wrong about many things. Over the years, I was routinely corrected and learned to discern essential differences between reality and fantasy, good and bad, worthwhile and worthless, right side up and upside down, light gray and dark gray. But the key point is this: Nothing I believe is original to me. My most core beliefs come from a cohesive primary source, the Word of God. I'm convinced of its veracity just as millions or possibly billions before me have been convinced in the same realities. So, what I believe is not my own assembled collection, but has been graciously delivered to me whole and tested. Is that just my interpretation of it? *But know this first of all, that no prophesy of Scripture is a matter of one's own interpretation, for no prophesy was ever made by an act of human will, but by men moved by the Holy Spirit spoke from God.* (2 Pet. 1:20-21)

Nothing I believe is original to me or innovative.

Wishing It's Such Doesn't Make It So

The dominant group-think today is that truth resides in the individual, so he or she can and must adventure within to discover it. This is typically done by incessant navel-gazing—a very short and boorish adventure! Today anything resembling a personal discovery or belief is supposed to be accepted as **fact**. One's self-verified interpretation is all that's required by others for them to give their nod of affirmation. And yet, should one of these nodders have a personal belief diametrically opposed to the original claimant, his or her belief is to be **also** given equal air time as "their truth."

And if that illogic and inconsistency is not enough madness, should a person dare hold firmly or teach a conviction rooted in long and widely-held beliefs (say... orthodox Christianity, sanctity of all life, creationism, only two genders, the law of non-contradiction), that person is popularly labeled narrow-minded, obsolete, or bigoted... and coldly dismissed.

Nevertheless, I shamelessly adopt and assert God's long-revealed Word as reality. *For the word of God is living and active, and sharper than any two-edged sword, even penetrating as far as the division of soul and spirit, of both joints and marrow, and able to judge the thoughts and intentions of the heart.* (Heb. 4:12)

This class is dismissed.

I Apologize ...but not like you think

#8

When someone says...

This life is all there is. There is nothing after this.

I apologize, but...

First off, that's a very ego-centric, short-sighted theory or guess. More specifically, it flies in the face of **all** the cultures and previous generations who have each contemplated some concept of life beyond this. The Scriptures reveal and affirm man's instinct: *God has made everything appropriate in its time. He has also set eternity in their heart....* (Eccl. 3:11) So, you or this generation that want to believe in "nothing" afterwards look suspiciously coincidental with this current culture that justifies whatever it wants to do and accepts no accountability... not even after death. The concept of annihilation after life is a cheap copout! It's comically ironic in light of all the contemporaneous chatter about respecting a nebulous worldwide humanity (multiculturalism), entertaining ideas of alternative realities, aliens, zombies, and especially embracing an anthropomorphized "Universe" that knows all!

As unpopular and old-fashioned as it may be today (which is a fairly good indicator that there's probably something to it), there will be a reckoning. *Therefore having overlooked the times of ignorance, God is now declaring to men that all people everywhere should repent, because He has fixed a day in which He will judge the world in righteousness....* (Acts 17:30-31) There **is** something after this life, and it's what **this** existence was all about.

The fool has said in his heart, "There is no God." (Psa. 14:1) The foolishness is this: He doesn't actually **believe** in nothing. His heart tells him there is something eternal, but like the toddler who hopes it all goes away by covering his eyes, he chooses to trick himself.

[And about that anthropomorphized "Universe"... check out #20.]

I Apologize ...but not like you think

#9

When someone says...

Evolution (macroevolution) is scientific fact.

I apologize, but...

Let me suggest, then, that it's like Apple Inc. They (Steve Wozniak & Steve Jobs) made the Apple 1 in 1976 and started selling it publicly in 1977. Then they kept researching and developing until they eventually came up with the MacBook Air in 2023. There are and have been really **only two** Apple computers, which are totally different in what they do and how they work. They have no relationship and nothing in common.

If you insist that that is nonsense and that the latter is an "evolution" of the former, I would ask for proof. How do you know that? You would undoubtedly point to **actual, existing, progressive generations** of Apple computers over 46 years, which is factual and logical.
Bravo!

So, I would point out that your scientific reasoning and proof is the existence of progressive generations (non-missing links) and you are right! Now, show integrity, be consistent, and apply the same scientific logic and proof requirement to the supposed strand connecting single-cell organisms, invertebrates, apes, and humans. None of the links exist, which is the **overwhelming non-evidence** of macroevolution. On the flip side, science has detected, measured, and touted **the ubiquitous existence of entropy** in every branch of experimentation, around every turn in our observable universe. And yet, a modern growing atheistic preponderance in the scientific community insists on a theory of evolution that flies in the face of that entropy. It's hard to know whether the absurdity or the audacity is more astounding!

It is only men's insistence of not acknowledging a Creator God that keeps the illogical, unscientific, false, and ludicrous narrative going.

#10

When someone says...

Good will win out over bad. There's a reason for whatever happens (a disappointment, delay, tragedy). It'll all work out.

I apologize, but...

That kind of vague optimism is a nice sentiment, but not much more than that. It sounds good, and people latch onto it and applaud those who preach it. The superficial and deceitful Joel Osteens capitalize on it. *Peace, peace! But there is no peace.* (Jer. 8:11) It's not reality... not in this life. Reality is more this way: *A poor wise man delivered a city by wisdom, but no one remembered that poor man. Wisdom is better than weapons of war, but one sinner destroys much good.* (Eccl. 9:13-18) *Man does not know whether it will be love or hatred; anything awaits him.* (Eccl. 9:1) Only in the coming Kingdom will things be set right, where wisdom, peace and goodness encompass all. The popularly quoted Romans 8:28 *God causes all things to work for good...* sounds similar on the surface but has at least two built-in deeper caveats:

1. *...to those who love God* - Loving God has many facets, but here's one not popularly accepted: Jesus said, *He who has my commandments and keeps them, he it is who loves me. And he who loves me will be loved by My Father who is in heaven.* Loving God is obeying God.

Wishing It's Such Doesn't Make It So

2. *...to those who are called according to His purposes -*
    His purposes, which He has communicated elsewhere
    in Scripture, are not the righting of this temporal world,
    this realm, but rather His eternal Kingdom. (Jn. 18:36; 1
    Jn. 2:15-16; Mt. 6:10)

One can grow to know the **character** of God and learn to love
Him... because God has chosen to reveal Himself thusly. *But
now that you have come to know God, or rather to be known
by God...* (Gal. 4:9); *This is eternal life, that they may know
You, the only true God, and Jesus Christ whom You have
sent.* (Jn. 17:3) But one cannot know the **actions** of God or
anticipate what He will do... because His ways are beyond
our comprehension and He has chosen to **not** reveal Himself
thusly. *You do not know the activity of God who makes all
things.* (Eccl. 11:5)

Will it all work out okay? God and life are just not that tame
and Disney-like. In the Narnia series, C. S. Lewis more aptly
captures God's character as Aslan the Lion: " 'Course he isn't
safe, but **he is good**. He is not a tame lion."

In **that** sense, yes, Good will win out over bad. But not without
some roaring!

I Apologize ...but not like you think

#11

When someone says...

Stop thinking binary! Everything is multi-faceted, possibilities endless, interpretations individualized. There are no absolutes.

I apologize, but...

The wisest man ever absolutely disagrees. His summarizing conclusion of his all-excelling research was this: *The conclusion, when all has been heard, is: fear God and keep His commandments, **because** this applies to every person. **For** God will bring every act to judgment, everything which is hidden, whether* (two options here) *it is **good or evil**.* (Solomon in Eccl. 12:13-14)

Despite the many freedoms, choices, and gray areas of life... all the acts of mankind will ultimately be revealed through perfect, sovereign judgment as binary. Binary terms ping-pong throughout the Bible:
- light & darkness
- day & night
- man & woman
- love & hatred
- sheep & goats
- good & evil
- alive & dead

Wishing It's Such Doesn't Make It So

- this life & the next
- heaven & hell

Then isn't the message of the Gospel actually good news for good people and bad news for bad people? No, the **message** is unary. *God... reveals the fragrance of the knowledge of Him in every place. For we* (the messengers of the Gospel) *are a fragrance of Christ to God among those who are being saved and among those who are perishing: to the one an aroma from death to death, to the other an aroma of life to life.* (2 Cor. 2:14-16) It's the **response** that's binary. One perfume, two noses.

Our culture's disdain for all things binary is not only ridiculously blind (can't recognize two genders!), but also evidence of its vehement rebellion against acknowledging the God Who will judge them. They don't like the smell of anything binary, especially a judgment, so they deny it... to their ruin. Yeah, I know it stinks... but only to some.

#12

When someone says...

Dystopias are just fiction, as are utopias.

I apologize, but...

Wrong on both accounts. It's understandable that the biblically illiterate or distrusting would conclude such, since so many fictional versions of dystopias and utopias have been formulated in books, movies, and around campfires by prepubescent boys. But once again, those of us graced with and steeped in the Scriptures know some coming -opias not otherwise known outside God's revelation.

In summary, there is a coming dystopia on earth that promises to be headed by a Beast, a man of lawlessness, who will bring to awful reality something worse than George Orwell's Big Brother or Max Tegmark's Prometheus fictionally did. That dystopia will be followed by both a utopia and a dystopia that never end. And we will all play roles in one of those latter two. We conceive of and play with ideas of dystopias and utopias **because** eternity and its realities have been seeded in every human heart. *He has made everything appropriate in its time. He has also set eternity in their heart, without which man will not find out the work which God has done from the beginning even to the end.* (Eccl. 3:1-11) Only those humble and wise enough to believe it will learn how to respond in time. And that's non-fiction.

[If you want to know more about how it all ends, read entry #3!]

#13

When someone says...

I'm not like most people. I'm different, kind of odd, even strange. I do my own thing.

I apologize, but...

Oh, so you're an average, contemporary American young person! As humans, we exhibit a common desire to be two seemingly divergent things – singular and included. We ache to be unique and individually significant. At the same time, we want to comfortably fit somewhere with others who will recognize and embrace us as one of them. All I can say to that observation made by mankind of mankind for millennia is, "I agree. I feel it and see it too." The two inclinations simultaneously exist. They represent reality. The question is then, "Are they contradictory and at odds, or complementary and fill out the other?" I believe the latter, that they correlate in a meaningful way... and for a wonder-filled reason!

Only God knows **why** He made us this way, but He goes out of His way to let us know these two desires are of His making. First, He tells us that each person was consciously created, **known** by Him before the foundations of the world. No matter what picture we might conjure in our minds of unique, individual significance, it has to pale in the face of that revelation! Second, we are made in His image in order to be a loved member of His royal, eternal family. Once again, it's hard to beat being of unending, warmly embraced, divine lineage. [Here are just a few passages of Scripture that reveal those facts:

Gen. 1:27-28; Eph. 1:3-4; 1 Cor. 13:11-12; Gal. 4:8-9; 1 Jn. 3:1-2; Eph. 2:17-19; 3:14-19] So, two seemingly opposing gut instincts turn out to be two potentially glorious realities!

Now, the catch! It's the word "potentially" above. It's each person's individual choice to recognize and embrace that grand plan or to reject it as fantasy. The choice is each person's. Our current culture is increasingly obsessed with being unique. The once productive, creative, adventuring character of our nation has devolved into a deteriorating, cliché, apathetic one that takes pride in being odd, a loner, directionless, quirky. More and more young people compare themselves to the endless barrage of worldwide possibilities on the Internet and in despondency resort to their basement to continue their unfruitful screen addiction. They have little foundational constitution compelling them to be anything meaningful or productive. So, instinctively responding to the two driving inclinations, they opt for a twisted version driven by meaninglessness and despair. They claim uniqueness, a different kind of sameness... just like everybody else. They retreat from society to join a disjoint "family" characterized by Halloween-like caricatures. (Just take a thoughtful look at today's everyday clothing, make-up, and body accessories, and tell me if it doesn't scream of twisted longing for attention.) To be known as deferring, humble, studious, virginal, or traditional is embarrassing. To be rebellious, proud, detached, shameless, edgy, or dark is applauded and reinforced.

Have you ever noticed and then wondered why one of the most popular tattoos, vehicle decals, jewelry art, and graffiti subjects is a skull? Of all the beautiful and pleasant things in this world, why is the symbol of a deceased, decayed, and detached human head so popular? If you've ever been around death, you know it's repulsive. Do the people sporting a skull want death close to them? Do they want to come home to find their child, spouse, or closest friend dead... to begin decaying into that detached skull? Have they even stopped to consider **why** they are attracted to such darkness? I doubt it. There is nothing healthy, pleasant, or even funny about it.

Woe to those who call evil good, and good evil; who substitute darkness for light and light for darkness; who substitute bitter for sweet and sweet for bitter! (Isa. 5:20)

Little is more sad and frightening than watching our seedling youth "grow up" ignorant of the **truly** unique essence and meaning-filled hope offered them. When self-destruction and empty pursuits become the normative path for our young people, one can only grieve inside and extend a pleading, "There **is** another Way!"

SECTION C:

KNEE-JERK ATTACKS ON TRADITIONAL VALUES

#14

When someone says...

You're racist. You're prejudiced. Are you prejudiced?

I apologize, but...

Of course I am. We all are. We are all naturally disposed by birth and upbringing toward our own kind (race, ethnicity, socio-economy, gender, etc.).

My early personal experience is common—a youthful unawareness of the culture in which I lived, my particular era, the specific attributes of my background, skin color, and opportunities. It was assumed to be normal. As I grew older, I began to notice differences and added some conscious evaluations—some informed and valid, some ignorant and invalid. Again, nothing uncommon here.

But becoming a Christian introduced a new frame of reference. In place of my own (as we all universally begin), I adopted God's frame of reference as mine. As Peter said, *I most certainly understand now that God is not one to show partiality, but in every nation the man who fears Him and does what is right is welcome to Him.* (Acts 10:34-35) In addition to a conscious effort to treat all men as peers, I also have a new source of love and tolerance from His Spirit within.

So, am I prejudiced? Sure, in almost every sphere of life. I notice differences and am prompted to place valuations on a person's age, his accent, her hairstyle, one's literary and music preferences, even a person's stride. Skin color, gender, and nationality are just obvious ones our culture likes to spotlight. I have prejudices for and against Turks, Guatemalans, Greeks, and Americans because I've lived among them. I have prejudices for and against Australians, Japanese, Brazilians, and Indians because I haven't lived among them. Some prejudice is due to knowledge. Some prejudice is due to ignorance. It's inescapable. What's important is how we choose to interact with those thoughts and what we volitionally do with them. Some of us learn by degrees to resist our biases, appreciate differences, and embrace others. I choose to embrace God's realities and directives as my perspective.

In our current, local, divisive culture, the terms prejudiced and racist have virtually no useful meaning. Picking and choosing prejudices has become arbitrary. But one thing is also gaining popularity—rejection and disdain of God's reality is the new norm; and a **true** Christian is the new "nigger".

I Apologize ...but not like you think

#15

When someone says...

Abortion—a woman has a right to her own body. It's ultimately her call.

I apologize, but...

Oh, but she certainly wouldn't want to shoulder that burden alone! And she shouldn't have to. Does she have the final say, the final and sole right to decide? If yes, that overrides the involved guy's rights in the decision, but then also his responsibility. They go hand-in-hand. Rights demand commensurate responsibilities in any sane system of justice. So, to be logically consistent, the same woman must take sole responsibility for the sex in which she chose to engage and the results. That includes the costs, any guilt, any medical errors, any regret... whatever. The guy involved is not responsible. Period. I can't imagine why a woman would accept that.

When the first woman, Eve, rebelled against God in the only prohibition He gave her, whom did God hold ultimately responsible? In the resulting fall of mankind, one could say both man and woman equally. But in terms of "blame", it fell even more on the man than on the woman. (Gen. 3) My point? I don't think women do themselves a favor when they insist on having the final or sole right to their bodies in an unwanted pregnancy. Illogically, they place the whole responsibility and blame on themselves, and remove it from the guy.

However, if she does not claim sole right, but shares it with the guy involved, then he not only shares equal right, but equal responsibility.

The preeminent fact is that they equally chose to engage in sex and **that** is the basis of who has responsibilities and rights, not the resulting pregnancy. The pregnancy is ancillary to the point. The sex had nothing **more** to do with the gal owning her body than it did the guy owning his body. If the argument is made that she had more at risk than he did, then she had more responsibility in the decision to have sex than he did, so she is more to "blame" for the unwanted consequences. Since it wasn't his body bearing the risk, he can argue that it was ultimately her choice, not his. If she argues that he **should** have been more concerned about her in the moment, then she has increased his responsibility, but therefore also his right to have an equal say in whether she has the abortion or not, and all that follows that decision as well. She can't play it both ways and be logically consistent. Was and is the sex **her** decision and choice, or was it **their** decision and choice? The rights and responsibilities must follow the answer consistently. The resulting pregnancy and subsequent decisions belong to whomever has the rights and responsibilities. God is just and righteous in His judgments. He does not impose another's guilt on us. Both the man and woman chose to have sex. **Both** are equally responsible and share equal rights.

An anticipated deflection often fed to women as ammo in the debate: What about in the case of pregnancy as a result of nonconsensual sex, rape, or incest? Raising those select circumstances resulting in pregnancy is a straw man argument, a comparatively tiny rarity (1.5%) used as excuse for the millions more free-choice abortions (98.5%). Answer the previous questions which affect the lion and lioness's share of millions of

I Apologize ...but not like you think

consensual sex pregnancies with integrity and consistency, and then one can possibly talk about the case of rape or incest.

Women under God's just and generous judgments should not fight for all the rights unless they want to stand before God with all the responsibility. God does not hold her accountable for the guy, so why should she take on that burden? *But everyone will die for his own iniquity; each man who eats the sour grapes, his teeth will be set on edge.* (Jer. 31:30)

One final plea. Should a woman say that the right to her body isn't a verdict between her and the guy, but between her and the baby, that's an even much more horrendous viewpoint. If one is so jaded to take that approach—the mother versus the baby— any amount of clear logic won't help her see things rightly.

This highly impassioned, literal life-and-death issue never will be settled with logic alone. It needs "poked in the eye," a re-boot. There is a better way all around. Embrace God's good and beautiful design for sex and marital relationship—one man and one woman for as long as they both shall live. *For this reason a man shall leave his father and mother, and be joined to his wife; and they shall become one flesh.* (Gen. 2:24) The Designer-Father knows best how to take care of His children. All of them.

#16

When someone says...

Unlimited gender types, gender neutral, gender fluid, intersex—they're all valid. You're homophobic. You're transphobic.

I apologize, but...

Absolutely, I'm thusly _____phobic. [Yes, I'm aware that the LGBTQQIP2SAAhahahahahaha... (Must I go on?) use of "-phobic" is a charged phraseology meant to be disparaging and instill fear of daring to disagree, but I'll accept the sophomoric derision if it helps clarify the issue.] One would have to be foolish to **not** be fearful (phobic) of such destructive perversion and irrationality. *A prudent person sees evil and hides himself, but the naive proceed and pay the penalty.* (Prov. 22:3) Of course I stand against newly invented "genders" which are based on feelings. **I reject fantasy as a determinant of life and lifestyle.** "Live not by lies." (Alexander Solzhenitsyn)

Let's make it simple enough, even for kids. Mr. Rogers' song on this topic will do the job quite nicely:

I Apologize ...but not like you think

Everybody's Fancy
Fred Rogers

Some are fancy on the outside
Some are fancy on the inside
Everybody's fancy
Everybody's fine
Your body's fancy and so is mine

Boys are boys from the beginning
Girls are girls right from the start
Everybody's fancy
Everybody's fine
Your body's fancy and so is mine

Only girls can be the mommies
Only boys can be the daddies
Everybody's fancy
Everybody's fine
Your body's fancy and so is mine

I think you're a special person
And I like your ins and outsides
Everybody's fancy
Everybody's fine
Your body's fancy and so is mine

The brevity and simplicity of this entry purposefully represents how **little** credence sane people should give to the claims and demands of the homosexual, transsexual, and all-things-gender agendas. But as to the **people** involved, they deserve the same loving offer of salvation as all men...and that which God pointedly directed to them: *Or do you not know that the unrighteous* *will not inherit the kingdom of God? Do not be deceived; neither fornicators, nor idolaters, nor adulterer, nor effeminate, nor homosexuals, nor thieves, nor the covetous, nor drunkards, nor revilers, nor swindlers, will inherit the kingdom of God. Such were some of you; but you were washed, but you were sanctified, but you were justified in the name of the Lord Jesus Christ and in the Spirit of our God.* (1 Cor. 6:9-11)

#17

When someone says...

Equality is the goal and equity is the means of accomplishing it. [applied to gender, race, handicaps, opportunity, socio-economics, socialism, etc.]

I apologize, but...

The premise of pan-equality is faulty, so the means of equity is consequently wrongheaded.

1. Equality in all or any category is neither possible nor desirable. The oldest and most foundational reality sets the precedence: There was, is, and will always be only one God who made many lesser things. All else are creations. All else necessarily follows that reality.
2. Equality already exists among some entities, but has valid inequalities inextricably attached. Men and women are equal God-image bearers, but own unequally innate, designed-in, physical and emotional attributes.
3. Valid attempts at equity are undermined by the overreach of those demanding equality indiscriminately. The history of non-stop warring in the world demonstrates mankind isn't satisfied with equality, but wants dominance, superiority, and revenge. *All things are wearisome; man is not able to tell it. The eye is not satisfied with seeing, the ear is not filled with hearing.*

(Eccl. 1:8) We like to ascribe "Just a little bit more" to only the John D. Rockefellers when asked "How much money is enough?", but it's actually systemic to human nature.

Most contemporary cries for equality by means of equity appear ill-informed or lacking integrity. When one denies the prime reality of one unique, sovereign God, it undermines the very ability to address the real problems caused by man's fallenness. Put simply, *the fear of the Lord is the **beginning** of wisdom.* (Prov. 1:9) All else **follows** that foundational start... or doesn't.

SECTION D:

JUST PLAIN SILLY SEMI-RELIGIOUS NOTIONS

I Apologize ...but not like you think

#18

When someone says...

You have to love yourself before you can love others.

I apologize, but...

We **all** automatically love and trust ourselves first and foremost. *No one ever hated his own flesh, but nourishes and cherishes it.* (Eph. 5:29) Ego, self, survival instinct, self-awareness are hardwired in all people from birth. A baby naturally wants what it wants. An adult **only potentially** learns to subdue that singular, innate, and top-priority urge through God-given revelation, instruction, and obedience to do **otherwise**. No one has to learn to be selfish or love oneself first. It is the human default response. The commonly cited examples of suicide, self-loathing, and low self-esteem are misnomers. They misdiagnose and conclude the absolute reverse of the core problem. The truth: Fear and anger at not feeling loved enough ("You are not loving me as much as I think I should be loved!") drives the twisted self-love to self-destructive responses. Possibly one of the more tragic illustrations of this confusion can be seen in the life and death of Whitney Houston. In her 1986 hit chart number one single she claimed this:
Because the greatest love of all is happening to me
I found the greatest love of all inside of me
*The greatest love of all **is easy to achieve***
Learning to love yourself, it is the greatest love of all

Just Plain Silly Semi-Religious Notions

After 26 years of singing and selling that refrain to millions of people, she was found drowned in her bathtub as a result of heart disease and cocaine use. The day before, her alleged last words were, "I just want to love and be loved." Such heartbreaking irony. And her last performed song two days before her death? *Jesus Loves Me*. She was right in that.

God is love. (1 Jn. 4:16) Only those who come to know Him and be healed by Him can enjoy their original design in love (the *Imago Deo* in Gen. 1:27), and then they can fully love others outside themselves.

As my former professor, Howard Hendricks, used to provocatively tell us, "You need the real disease before you can infect others."

I Apologize ...but not like you think

#19

When someone says...

Loving all is the goal. You're not loving, but a hater because you don't accept _____.

I apologize, but...

Love is not indiscriminate. It is not a blank check written to anyone at any time for anything. If it were, it would be empty, hollow. True love unquestionably discriminates, first and foremost, between truth and fantasy. Next it distinguishes light and darkness, good and evil. The most simple and ubiquitous example is that of a tiny child wanting things harmful (poison or a predator) or lacking required maturity (to walk in the street or drive the car). Imagine being an adult and telling a little child that it's okay to touch a rattlesnake or play in the street! Sometimes we best love by countering, correcting, restricting, and, yes, disciplining.

Love (Greek *agape*), as God its Designer unveils it, might be defined as:

> **Love**: *noun – a determined act of the will that earnestly seeks the other's highest good*

That definition incorporates resolve, action, conscious decision, heart motivation, effort, and selflessness. That's a far cry from the limp, toothless, extemporaneous feeling so freely passed off as love these days. Our current culture has a definition so broad

66

and inconsistent, it's literally (in the original sense of the word, meaning "literally") meaningless. One could compact today's convoluted definition of love as:

Love: noun, verb, particip... whichever of those grammar thingies it is – accepting everything and everyone indiscriminately... unless it threatens what I want to believe is true or right, then I'm against it and can be justifiably hateful as my expression of love

Yes, I know definitions aren't usually written in the first person singular, but **this** one absolutely needs to be!

*Little children, let us not **love** with word or with tongue, but in deed and truth.* (1 Jn. 3:18) Telling someone a falsehood or affirming their fantasy just because it agrees with their feelings or relieves them of adult responsibility is **not** loving them.

What the Christian knows and has the power to do is to simultaneously love the sinner and hate the sin. *Have mercy on some, who are doubting; save others, snatching them out of the fire; hating even the garment polluted by the flesh.* (Jude 1:23)

In contrast, a world being unable to discern between truth and fantasy doesn't result in love, but in something quite different with hateful outcomes. *Do not be surprised, brothers and sisters, if the world hates you.* (1 Jn. 3:13) "The more a society drifts from the truth, the more it will hate those who speak it." - George Orwell

The truly loving thing some people need from others is to have a truly grown-up someone give them an unwavering "No."

#20

When someone says...

I believe that the Universe knows, controls and determines all.

I apologize, but...

So then, what or who is the Universe? If you can't define it or if you claim that it's indefinable, then you are merely guessing and lost in terms of any foundation for living—a total crapshoot. However, if you claim characteristics of any kind for the Universe, let me ask, "How do you **know** that?" Ultimately, the postulates are your selective compilation of man's ideas and the conclusions your own. You are, in fact, the god of your own designed religion, and therefore, are personally and completely responsible for everything that happens in your life.

For perspective, there are currently 8 billion-plus people living in the world (and popular science guesstimates over 100 billion already deceased!). So, what are the odds that your individually conjured up, personally designed religion or philosophy is correct, truth, reality of what actually is? About 1 in 8 billion. Good luck with that. Better yet, consider what you're wagering. *There is a way which seems right to a man, but its end is the way of death.* (Prov. 14:12)

#21

When someone says...

You can't understand what I'm going through because you've never _____." [been gay, lost a child, struggled with addiction, been poor, etc.]

I apologize, but...

That's not exactly true. The truth is that the God-Man, Jesus Christ, **does** understand—and perfectly. *All things came into being through Him, and apart from Him not even one thing came into being that has come into being.* (Jn. 1:3-4) He not only made us, He became one of us. You may have heard that but it seems distant and irrelevant to the very real, skin-in-the-game issues you mentioned. And how does that apply to a mere person like me being able to understand your need? Here's the part that many people don't know. Christians aren't limited to their own experiences and knowledge. In an amazing Scripture we are told: *For who has known the mind of the Lord, that he will instruct Him? But* **we** (Christians) **have** *the mind of Christ.* (1 Cor. 2:16) I may not be able to wholly empathize with you, but that doesn't mean I don't have access to the mind of God that certainly **is** sufficient for your every need. Don't trust me. But do trust Him... even if He tells you through me that you can!

#22

When someone says...

My faith, my Christianity, is a personal thing.

I apologize, but...

If you design it, then **you** are the god of your faith and responsible for everything that happens, including all your lifelong or eternal consequences. All of them! There is no one you can blame or hold responsible for anything done against you. And commensurate with your role as originator of your religion, you should not be ashamed of claiming to be deity or be offended by my inference that you are, in fact, a god.

However, if you claim your belief is still Christianity, then I simply point out to you that Christianity has always held this tenet: *There is one body and one Spirit, just as also you were called in one hope of your calling; one Lord, one faith, one baptism, one God and Father of all who is over all and through all and in all.* (Eph. 4:4) *For just as the* (human) *body is one and yet has many parts, and all parts of the body, though they are many, are one body, so also is Christ.* No part can rightly say *I have no need of you.* (1 Cor. 12:12, 21)

That doesn't leave room for a personally designed, interpreted, or lived-out Christianity. You either learn what God's Word says and embrace it, or you are not Christian. Sorry, it's not a personal thing.

#23

When someone says...

If you believe enough, you can do anything. You just have to have faith.

I apologize, but...

This may be the most meaningless and inane sentiment I regularly hear these days from popular movies, songs, and average people trying to sound deep and thoughtful. If they'd actually **think**, even momentarily, they might realize how utterly empty of content the idea is. Despite the fact that every Disney movie's message and catchy anchor song circles around to this theme, it is stupefying that anyone but simple children repeat it! But the average collegian spouts it as if it meant something.

Dare I analogize when following simple logic these days seems impossible for many folks? Imagine the following conversation:

Abbey: *I feel a little lost and directionless.*
Zeb: *You just need to fight.*
Abbey: *Fight what?*
Zeb: *Just fight as hard as you can.*
Abbey: *For or against whom or what?*
Zeb: *It doesn't matter, as long as you're fighting with all you have to give.*
Abbey: *But I don't have anything or anyone I want to fight.*
Zeb: *The important thing is to be fighting and not quitting*

no matter what.
Abbey: *But what will it accomplish if I don't know what or whom or why?*
Zeb: *You can win anything and everything if you just fight.*
Abbey: *But I have nothing to fight for or against.*
Zeb: *That's irrelevant. Fighting is both the process and the goal! Get it?*
Abbey: *Not even in the slightest.*
Replace "fight" with "believe" or "have faith" and you have the mindless mantra of our day.

People, especially young people, have adopted the claim that believing apart from an object of belief is something... which it's not... not any more than fighting is something without an object or purpose for which to fight. It only becomes a real fight when there is something or someone to fight for or against. Shadow boxing scores no points. Belief in belief is like fighting for fighting. It's meaningless. It's a subject without an object. It's eating without food, breathing in a vacuum, adding without numbers... (here we go) texting without a device!

If you're still not convinced that belief in belief is nothing, let me offer this mental exercise: **Believe you don't believe.**

[If "I believe in myself" is the answer you'd give in response to the above Apology, let me suggest you read #2 & #22. If "I don't believe in anything" is your response, then give #8 a try.]

SECTION E:

POPULAR BUT WRONG IDEAS ABOUT CHRISTIANITY

#24

When someone says...

The Christian message is so negative and pessimistic. Sin, repenting, lost people, hell... really?

I apologize, but...

As popular as it is today to promote optimism and positive thinking, that doesn't change reality. The unscrubbed answer is this: The future of our current world **is** pessimistic. It ends in destruction. But, the future of the eternal world is optimistic... for those who embrace and cooperate with God's reality. When Christians are negative or pessimistic, it's typically because they're addressing the stuff of our **current** world with its daily demise and inevitable ruin. It leads me personally, at times, to genuine sorrow and aching. Solomon's accurate insight forced him to describe this world "under the sun" by saying *All things are wearisome.... In much wisdom is much grief; in increased knowledge is increased pain.* (Eccl. 1:8, 18) He was seeing things as they are. The apostle Paul wasn't exaggerating or talking about just **some** Christians when he said *Through many tribulations we must enter the kingdom of God.* (Acts 14:22) The path to God is a rugged and difficult one. Anyone who tells you otherwise is either misled or selling you a different gospel. Of that, Paul was once again very clear: *But even if we or an angel from heaven should preach to you a gospel contrary to what we have preached to you, he is to be accursed!* (Gal. 1:6)

The solid preacher C. H. Spurgeon got it right—"There is nothing in this world to foster a Christian's piety, but everything to destroy it."

The Gospel is and literally means "good news", but the hope of that wonderful message isn't chiefly for our 80 or 90 years of life here and now. However, when it comes to the kingdom to come, I couldn't be more positive about *Things which eye has not seen and ear has not heard, and which have not entered the heart of man, all that God has prepared for those who love Him.* (1 Cor. 2:9)

I Apologize ...but not like you think

#25

When someone says...

It's the exclusivity of Christianity with which I disagree. Religion should be inclusive. Besides, all religions are basically the same and have the same goals at heart.

I apologize, but...

Everything about those statements is wrong:

- First off, the claim and support of inclusiveness is just parroting the popular cultural chorus without really giving it thought. No one really wants inclusiveness across the board. Do you want everyone to have inclusive access to your house, income, spouse, children, car, your country's border, law-making, power grid, and most importantly... your iPhone and passwords, regardless of their character or intensions?
- In fact, it is almost exclusively religion that you want to be inclusive because you want possible benefits (blessed, saved, virtue?) without restrictions or commitment.
- If anything, religion should be *exclusive* because it distinguishes truth from falsehood, reality from fantasy. If one has faith in **anything**, it should be reality. Christianity is simply claiming to communicate to mankind **reality** (the practical essence of the word "truth") from his Creator.

- It is accurate that the religions of the world are alike in a few basic matters. All express some common morality, which always includes a form of the golden rule. But most obvious and prominent is a merit basis for reaching what ever is their perceived goal (heaven, bliss, absorption into the cosmos, deification, etc.). There is measurement, assessment, and results. Christianity is truly separate and unique in that it is **not** merit based. It is the offer of relationship with the Divine including a knowledge of forgiveness now in this life based solely on the merit of Jesus Christ, the initiator and end of all life. No other religion even remotely approximates that scenario and message.
- And finally, the "exclusivity" statement applied to Christianity reveals an ignorance of Christianity's most outstanding and unique claim: Salvation has been offered with universal *inclusiveness*—Christ died and raised **for all mankind**. (1 Pet. 3:18) It is **mankind** who has and makes the choice to accept and receive that offer, or not. To reject Christianity is to exclude yourself from God's universally inclusive **offer**.

You might want to re-think what you **really** believe and want.

#26

When someone says...

Why can't Christians accept others' beliefs also and just get along with those who believe differently?

I apologize, but...

But they **are**... in masses! In most church groups, you have what you've asked. The contemporary church has largely listened to that charge by the world and conceded its core beliefs and values. As Voddie Baucham opines, they have added and embraced an Eleventh Commandment that trumps the original Ten—***Thou shalt be nice.***

Despite conventional *Precious Moments* sentimentalism, **Jesus was not nice**. To His beloved followers and an eventual prominent leader among the Apostles, Peter, he roared these words: *Get behind Me, Satan!* When Jesus gives this shocking rebuke to Peter, allying him with Satan, He explained, *for you are not setting your mind on God's interests, but **man's**.* (Mk. 8:31-38) Jesus regularly pointed out and taught about man's worldly ways, but his most stinging rebukes and not-so-precious-moments of righteous anger (calling Pharisees a *brood of vipers* and *white-washed tombs*; braiding and brandishing a whip and upending tables in the Temple) were reserved for those applying worldly notions to religious matters. Peter was confronting Jesus based on his own religious ideas of what a Messiah should be doing! Ironically, this interchange took place immediately after Peter made the admirable and spot-on declaration, *You are the Christ*. "Man's ways" are always counter to God's ways, but they're most damning when unholy alliances are attempted between the kingdoms of men and the Kingdom of God. Certainly, sins like adultery, theft, and slander harm people and ruin lives, but they don't irreversibly consign people to eternity apart from God. But... replacing the saving plan of the Kingdom of God with the short-sighted and impotent religious plans of men does. And **that** draws out the impassioned, **love-based wrath** of the Savior. *Get behind Me, Satan!*

Today's quasi-spiritual world demands a kinder, gentler religion, emasculated and ashamed of real crosses, while prizing feigned peace instead of confronting the world with Truth. Many claiming Christ are bit-by-bit joining you, the world, in all matters and substituting outward niceness for inward lovingkindness, even among their fellow "believers". They have learned to smile at each other, stop confronting sin within, and have given holy ground to those outside... literally, by saying "all are welcome." But, now that you've won that acceptance, don't expect to necessarily find deep, committed, faithful relationships. Being nice is not the same thing as the *agape* love and fellowship with the Father, Son and Spirit that was to inspire their corporate fellowship. Or to put it as Rich Mullins did: *These people are friendly, but they'll never be your friend.*

Be careful what you ask for!

#27

When someone says...

You're not to judge others. You can't know what's in people's hearts.

I apologize, but...

It's amusing that this verse is one non-Christians love to quote. It's one of a few dislodged "gotcha" verses they have in their arsenal to deflect Christians whose words strike home. As usual, when non-Christians use the Word, they misuse it.

The rightness or wrongness of judging has everything to do with the preparedness, accuracy, and motive of the Christian, not with a blanket do or don't. The full teaching of Jesus around this beloved quote (Mt. 7:1-28) discloses that fact. Jesus' words were: *Do not judge, so that you will not be judged.* His warning is to not judge unless we are prepared to be judged by the same measure. He then continues to teach several situations and ways in which to judge rightly. He tells us to judge ourselves first, then judge others as is needed and possible. In fact, we must be able to do it and do it well in order to be mature Christians! We must judge others on a daily basis in order to discern how we relate to them. And because of the illuminating light we have from God's Word and Spirit, most of the time it's straight-forward who is who and what is what. After the warning about judging others, Jesus continues, *Beware of the false prophets... you will know them by their fruits... Therefore everyone who hears these words of mine and acts on them, may be compared to a wise man....* Jesus says it's a wise man who learns to judge rightly.

The Apostle John likewise teaches (1 Jn. 3:4-10) about us being able to judge who is who and the source of people's inspiration and power: *Little children, make sure no one deceives you; the one who practices righteousness is righteous, just as He* (Jesus) *is righteous; the one who practices sin is of the devil.* In order to not be deceived, we're told that we can discern or judge **other people's** character and master. And if that isn't enough, he follows by instilling confidence in these judgments. *By this the children of God and the children of the devil are obvious.* He says it's not that hard to tell—their practices make it patently clear. *The one who does good is of God; the one who does evil has not seen God.* (3 Jn. 1:11) Not only do we judge, we do it with clarity because we start conscientiously with ourselves before God. And then, we also do it with insight and confidence because, as Paul says, *we have the mind of Christ.* (1 Cor. 2:16)

Many times when someone charges us with judging, ironically, they are judging what we have done or said. Unwittingly, it's what prompted them to pluck out that particular ill-used phrase *Judge not.* If they only knew that Christians could rightly respond by quoting 1 Cor. 6:3 *Do you not know that we will judge angels? How much more matters of this life.*

#28

When someone says...

Christians believe money is the root of all evils. That's a bit extreme!

I apologize, but...

First off, that's a misquote of the original, which in its correct exactness is more revealing and much less easy to toss off as ridiculously simplistic.

*If we have food and covering, with these we shall be content. But those who want to get rich fall into a temptation and a snare and many foolish and harmful desires which plunge men into ruin and destruction. For **the love of money is a root of all sorts of evil**, and some by longing for it have wandered away from the faith and pierced themselves with many griefs.* (1 Tim. 6:9-10)

Not money, but **the love of money** is the focus of concern. Most people, Christian or non-Christian, would claim they don't love it. Then I would ask those who deny it concerns them, "How do you know? How much have you deeply questioned the possibility for yourself? Do you love money?" Try this test for starters. To which of the following have you given more thought and energy:

1) How can I gain more money?

2) How is gaining money affecting my heart?
Your honest answer might be telling. So, how much **should** a person think about gaining money? Here's Solomon's answer to that question: *Do not weary yourself to gain wealth. **Cease from your consideration of it.*** (Prov. 23:4) Ceasing doesn't allow much time put toward it—in fact, none.

As a Christian attempting to honestly evaluate my heart in relationship to God and money, many years ago I gave myself this standard of measure: **Never let money be the bottom line in any decision.** I can already hear a buzz of dissention. "That's not realistic or practical... it's impossible in the real world... that's an overreaction to a real problem... let's be reasonable.... And from Christian friends I can hear, "That's way too legalistic" followed by the popular biblical *coup d'état* that's supposed to answer all arguments and relieve all guilt concerning money—"It's all about stewardship."

To all those objections and more, I would respond that I have arduously entertained those arguments which defend the love of money in any sense (that **is** what we're talking about here), and would follow again with the question, "Have you?" If so, Christian, what do you do with these words of Jesus? *No one can serve two masters; for either he will hate the one and love the other, or he will be devoted to one and despise the other. You cannot serve God and wealth.* (Mt. 6:24) I recommend you invest as much time in meditating on this Scripture as you put into... let's see... the management of your finances?

SECTION F:

CONFUSION ABOUT THE CHURCH

#29

When someone says...

The church should be seeker friendly, welcoming and accepting of all kinds of people.

I apologize, but...

It's not friendly to deceive people. It's not typically genuine seekers who become attracted when Christians take that approach. The Church is to be comprised of those *called out* of the world *in repentance* to be radically saved and different from the world. Here is one of Paul's instructions to church leaders as to what should characterize their preaching: *Preach the Word. Be ready in season and out of season; **correct, rebuke, and exhort** with great patience and instruction.* (2 Tim. 4:2) From experience I can assure you that even when done *with great patience and instruction* as Paul says, it will **not** be seeker friendly to faithfully *correct, rebuke, and exhort* from the Word of God. Trying to attract people to a "world-friendly church" (now that's a contradiction of terms! 1 Jn. 2:15-16) is to attempt winning them through deceit, bait-and-switch, or ignorance of the Church's nature. It miscommunicates the Gospel to the lost while compromising the need of the saved people within. It attracts those wanting the world but with a religious pass to heaven or some other less eternal motive. A. W. Tozer insightfully truncated the point: "You win them **to** what you win them **with**."

Here is the rest of Paul's charge quoted above: *For a time will come when they will not tolerate sound doctrine; but wanting to have their ears tickled, they will accumulate for themselves teachers in accordance with their own desires, and they will turn their ears away from the truth and turn aside to myths.* (2 Tim. 4:3-4) There it is—as accurate a picture of today's seeker friendly church as one could expect to see! The end result is not the Church, but something led by hired entrepreneurs, tickling, falsely palatable, mythical, worldly. It is neither "seeker" nor "friendly".

#30

When someone says...

The church will prevail regardless. God says so. I will build My church and the gates of Hades will not overpower it. (Mt. 16:18)

I apologize, but...

Yes, if you mean by that:
- The TRUE Church, which God alone builds and knows, will endure.
- The INVISIBLE Church, not made of brick and mortar, will be established.
- The HEAVENLY Church, not built with earthly strategies and world-appealing means, will multiply.
- The HOLY Church, hated by the world, will live rejected, separated, and persecuted like her Groom and Master was.
- The SINGULAR Church, unlike false religions and religious "churchianity" (loyalty to the church rather than to Christ), will be small, narrow, unpopular, few, struggling, rare.

The ETERNAL Church, unlike the great number of misdirected man-made fellowships and institutions, will be separated, recognized, loved, preserved and welcomed by Her Author and Perfecter, Jesus, for eternity.

Yes, **that** Church will prevail.

Confusion About The Church

#31

When someone says...

Doctrinal statements are essential for churches, denominations, para-church organizations.

I apologize, but...

Such doctrinal statements are merely tools, and by definition not complete canons of belief. A tool can be well made or poorly made. A tool can be used well or poorly used. The early Church strenuously labored during its initial few hundred years to establish creeds to help guard and guide the Church from infancy to maturity, from heresy and into orthodox, faithful belief. The result was a very few, succinct statements (i.e., Apostles', Nicene creeds). About the only things the following couple of millennia have contributed are volume, error, and division. In the name of specificity and clarity, endless statements have been proffered. They prove largely useless and divisive. The specificity and clarity were already available... in their **source** document... the Bible. Those initial painfully compressed creeds were not perfect but had **value in their accurate brevity**. To expand on them could only be improved by reverting them back to the whole of their source, the unabridged written Revelation of God to man that truly is sufficient for all things. (2 Tim. 3:16-17; 2 Pet. 1:3-4)

Recent doctrinal statements have proved to be lesser. A few go for more conciseness, creating overly simplistic dogma or opening up interpretations galore because of overly broad parameters. The overwhelming majority, however, go for more length and specificity, codifying as "essential" details that truly require the whole counsel of Scripture, not just a lengthier redress. We don't need more or better-tailored doctrinal statements or creeds. We need God's people firmly established on the only essential Foundation. *For no man can lay a foundation other than the one which is laid, which is Christ Jesus.* (1 Cor. 3:10-11) Only the **whole** of the revealed, living Word is sufficient. **He** cannot be condensed.

Confusion About The Church

#32

When someone says...

The church is here to change the world. It should fight evil and promote good. [mainly promulgated by believers as "bringing in the Kingdom"]

I apologize, but...

Jesus delineated a **different** kingdom view in His teaching: *My kingdom is not of this world.* (Jn. 18:36) As His followers personally live out His kingdom values during their earthly years, they will add redeeming elements and some sanity amidst the general, protracted fall of mankind. The ultimate good they are charged with spreading is nothing short of the Gospel, which trumps and imbues all other good works. However, they were not called to nor will they be able to bring kingdom perfection about here on this earth, in this era.

Both Roman Catholicism and some Protestant camps have contributed to a faulty expectation of an eventual moral, godly Kingdom on this earth. Although Roman Catholics believe mankind is sinful, they wrongly believe **all** people have latent goodness in them, that even non-believers and other religionists are seeking God, and the majority of them will eventually turn to the Truth of God. Tragically, that doesn't square with what God says about mankind. *There is none righteous, not even one; there is none who understands, there is none who* *seeks for God.* (Rom. 3:10-11) Catholics' idea that religious rituals serve to fan the flame of innate love for God into life even among non-believers is totally on its head. One can squeeze the bellows over cold, dead ashes all day long, but they don't blaze into fire. The spark of life only begins when God re-creates it anew; thus He poignantly told the religionist Nicodemus, *Truly, truly, I say to you, unless one is born again he cannot see the kingdom of God.* (Jn. 3:3)

Similarly, Protestants who hold to a Post-Millennial kingdom believe that a Gospel-inspired humanity will eventually dominate the earth, making it nearly perfect and readied for Jesus' Kingly return. That fantasy is so world-inspired and flies in the face of so many Scriptures (to cite just a few: Rom. 3:5-28; 2 Tim. 3:1-5; Rev. 21:1), it's almost laughable, if it wasn't so heartbreakingly disastrous!

In this context, "world" rightly defined is "the world" of the Scripture, which has this succinct enjoinment and description: *Do not love the world nor the things in the world. If anyone loves the world, the love of the Father is not in him. For all that is in the world, the lust of the flesh and the lust of the eyes and the boastful pride of life, is not from the Father, but is from the world. The world is passing away, and also its lusts, but the one who does the will of God lives forever.* (1 Jn. 2:15-16)

And, *Do you not know that friendship with the world is hostility toward God? Therefore whoever wishes to be a friend of the world makes himself an enemy of God.* (Jas. 4:4)

The world makes endless problems that will not ever be completely arrested and will ultimately bring it down to ruin and destruction by God (not global warming). I am **for** many things and **against** many things by nature of being established in His

Truth. But I will never eradicate the many things I am against (abortion, legal injustice, big business greed, immorality dominating the arts, pornography, LGBTQ+ & trans madness, educational demise, exploitation by big pharma, poisoning by processed food Goliaths, etc.). I will never be able to bring about global rightness (unprejudiced love, equality, mercy, compassion, selfless generosity, solve world hunger, etc.).

Kingdom perfection is not the destiny of **this** world. It is for the **next** world. So that is our message, the Gospel (= good news). Even though we rightly pray as Jesus taught us, *Thy kingdom come, Thy will be done on earth as it is in heaven* (Mt. 6:10), we are not here to bring about the Kingdom of God on earth. We are here to bring the Kingdom of heaven's message in word and life to a dying and doomed world in order that they might believe and exchange hope in this short earthly life for the offered eternal heavenly one.

The sobering message and outcome for the people of this world?
Enter through the narrow gate; for the gate is wide and the way is broad that leads to destruction, and there are many who enter through it. For the gate is small and the way is narrow that leads to life, and there are few who find it. (Mt. 7:13-14)

#33

When someone says...

Women in the church are way behind those outside. They're still second-class citizens, doormats, suppressed.

I apologize, but...

That impression is exactly what those outside the Church, and especially major media, want you to believe. Most who say that have never bothered to ask women in the Church if that's how they feel. If they did, they'd learn that the overall contentment factor for women in the Church is much higher than for those outside. [There have been numerous studies done to measure that sort of thing, with the great majority revealing that Christian women have greater satisfaction, especially marital, than non-Christian ones.] So, with a little embarrassment and compromise, I'll borrow a psychological term and suggest you may be "projecting".

When the Church holds to the teachings of the Bible for the roles of women in the Church setting and in the human family (both of which it does clearly address), women have a very honorable and satisfying role. Probably the best corroborating evidence is not to defend them, but to instead describe women in our current culture **outside** the Church. The recent few generations of the ever-escalating push for women's rights and "equality" with men has magnificently backfired. Women's access to the boardroom and escape from the home front have neither fulfilled them through the former nor relieved them from the latter. The mash-up in the commercial sector has them battling with more men, only the men are outwardly restrained for fear of being sued or labeled chauvinists, and have retreated into more feminized ways of dealing with it. Try to find a healthy, secure, honest man who **prefers** his boss being a woman. The mishmash of roles at home still has women exhausted trying to pay for and coordinate with childcare stand-ins. The kids are a mess, infidelity skyrockets while marriage plummets, therapy for everyone is normative, general health is declining despite modern medicine, abuse of all stripes pounds harder, and... women are not happier, contented, peaceful. And for what it's worth, neither are the men.

Can I prove those generalizations? I don't have to. They're so patently evident for someone objectively observing our culture. But don't take my word for it. I'm just a Christian man. Ask a Christian woman.

SECTION G:

SKEWED IDEAS CHRISTIANS SOMETIMES HOLD

#34

When someone says...

Why do Christians blindly support Israel? The Jews killed Jesus!

I apologize, but...

It's a good question. Let me add a few more to it. Why does an ancient nation like Israel still exist? Why is little Israel always in the news and a locus of interest? Why are there so many influential Jews in finance, arts, industry, etc.? Why the protracted antisemitism? Those questions should raise even more intrigue to the query! It's long and involved, but let me try a few synthesizing stabs at the whole thing.

* The Jews were a nation formed by God from a small, no-account people descended from a shepherd named Abraham for a specific role in His grand plan; namely, they were to be His witnesses to mankind and the gene-pool into which he would plant His Savior-seed, Jesus. That partly answers why they are so influential—they think they're somebody special and aren't afraid to act on it. *Chutzpah!* They also have a special "X Factor" blessing from God that apparently often blesses everything from their artistic résumé to their bank accounts. *Berakah!* Unfortunately, they got spiritually cocky and abandoned the most important Factor in their history—their God! Important observation: God isn't unfaithful just because His people are.

Skewed Ideas Christians Sometimes Hold

* As His chosen people for this purpose, God made promises to them that they would play a role in the earth's drama all the way to the final scene, **even if** they weren't faithful... which they haven't been. **That** answers why they're still around in the news today, unlike other ancient by-gone peoples such as the Hittites, Babylonians, or Romans for that matter, even though they sanctioned the Jews killing God's very own Jewish-Savior-Son, Jesus. Another flip-side insight into Jehovah: God keeps His promises even when His people don't. He isn't reactionary and doesn't have to make adjustments in response to man's failures.

* The fact that antisemitism has been a resurfacing theme for millennia should make us wonder at the crosshairs of attention on such a small people group. Of all the earth's tongues, tribes, peoples, and nations, why does a country the size of New Jersey attract so much vitriol over centuries? We may have already partly answered that question. Here's a people telling everyone that they are God's unique, select nation, flaunting their undeniably impressive skills and blessings, and yet much of the time acting utterly contrary to their claimed teachings about humility, generosity, morality, honesty, etc. On top of that, instead of being the *light to the nations* (Isa. 42:6; 49:6) they were chosen to be, they double-down on the "we're in and you're out" message. Yeah, that would generate some bad taste in the mouth of the world's *Goyim*.

* Many Christians are not biblically knowledgeable and make a huge misstep in assuming political Israel is spiritual Israel. God clearly tells Christians that *It is not as though the word of God has failed. For they are not all Israel who are descended from Israel; nor are they all children of God because they are Abraham's descendants... that is, it is not the chil-*

dren of the flesh who are children of God, but children of the promise are regarded as descendants. (Rom. 9:6-8) That's it in a nutshell. Being born in a garage doesn't make you a car. Cutting to the chase, only Jews who embrace Jesus as the Jewish Messiah for the whole of humanity are true Jews; the rest are just physical descendants of Abraham, which carries no weight on eternal scales. Many Christians take the verses that say of Israel, *And I will bless those who bless you, and the one who curses you I will curse* (Gen. 12:3; 27:29; Num. 24:9), and wrongly apply them to political Israel of today, instead of those few Jews who have recognized Jesus for who He is, their Messiah.

That's the skinny on why so many Christians naively support anything "Israel" does today.

But finally... the good news! The same Bible reveals that as the end of time approaches, because of God's faithfulness there will be a groundswell of Jews who turn to Jesus and will fulfill God's plan in the Kingdom to come. (Rom. 11, esp. 26-27) Now, **that** is worthy of a loud, raucous, Hebrew *Hallelujah!*

#35

When someone says...

Missionaries are special Christians—either super spiritual or a little weird and can't fit in their own culture.

I apologize, but...

There are a lot of myths about missionaries and missions work to foreign lands that the American church perpetuates. As is often the case, these myths tend to represent the polar extremes:

Myth of the super saint vs. the oddball – Some people put them on a spiritual pedestal expecting near miraculous lives, fruit, and endurance beyond the "average Christian". Others assume it's the quirky and unsophisticated who should "go overseas" since they don't fit here, but their oddity won't be as noticeable "over there". The truth is that the requirements of ministry cross-culturally involve so many additional challenges beyond those in one's own culture, the call demands and deserves deeply grounded servants of Christ—nothing more, nothing less.

Myth of the hungry heart vs. the hardened heathen – Some believe foreigners (the target audience of missionaries' efforts), especially less educated ones, will be hungry for the Gospel and prove to be low-hanging fruit. Others expect

103

the followers of idolatrous religions to be hardened and dangerous. The truth is that all people, whether educated or not, fight the same lusts and pride common to mankind, and struggle to embrace the gracious salvation offered by God; but a few will!

Myth of the movement vs. routine – Some have heard of missionary movements and "waves" that place all the responsibility on whether the Spirit is moving or not right now. Others naively believe the work of the Gospel will get done in the world as we just do our own local Christian living. The truth is that the Great Commission to go and make disciples (Mt. 28:19-20) is for all times and necessitates real Christians preparing for real cross-cultural labor among real different peoples and places... or the work of the Gospel suffers. At the same time, there have been observable eras and places of extraordinary reception and rejection. The Spirit does move in mysterious ways.

Myth of the staple vs. the dessert – Some think foreign missions is what it's all about. Others think it's an intriguing optional novelty. The truth is that God does love the whole world and we are one small slice. We either embrace His universal heart or we don't.

Western culture has played an impressive role in the propagation of the message of Christ worldwide over the first two thousand years. However, our current, specific brand of Western culture is so individualistic, immature, shallow, and fleshly, I fear that our participation in the Great Commission may be fairly judged, as Dallas Willard labels it, the Great Omission.

#36

When someone says...

Ecclesiastes is depressing. Solomon was a mess.

I apologize, but...

No, Ecclesiastes is reality. And Solomon was what God said he was—the wisest mere human ever. And wisdom begins with a fear of the Lord. So, although Solomon had some significant failings, even those experiences were part of the unique role he was specially designed by God to fulfill. Writing the book of Ecclesiastes and many Proverbs for us was the passed-on fruit of all he experienced. No, his life doesn't fit into a nice, neat package we can label "good" or "bad", but he was no fool or lost soul. (2 Sam. 7:12-15)

Ecclesiastes offers invaluable wisdom for enjoying the best and dealing with the worst of life *under the sun*, this life on earth. One of several mini-conclusions in the looping message of the book (Eccl. 7:12-14) says that God alone knows and sovereignly controls the future. We do not. In the meantime, it's a temporal advantage **to live in concert with Him** during this life under the sun. **That's called wisdom**. If God "bends" anything differently than we might have wanted or expected, we can't "fix" it otherwise. When something in this bent world needs straightening (like a life), only God can accomplish it. So, enjoy the prosperity. Seriously consider the adversity. Know

I Apologize ...but not like you think

there's a God behind it all who perfectly and justly sorts it out. Wisdom upon wisdom is offered through God's chosen man, Solomon.

And what about Solomon's repeated phrase, *Vanity of vanities, all is vanity!*? (Eccl. 1:2) This repeated lament speaks of the limited sphere of this life on earth. It's temporary and testing. None of it remains. It's not until the last two verses that the book finally addresses life outside this known one. God had Solomon write a book to mankind concentrating on life *under the sun.* Why? I have some ideas, but I don't know for sure—I'm not that wise. But I have a sneaking suspicion that Solomon was!

#37

When someone says...

Do you think that person is saved?

I apologize, but...

I can't know. I have only their word and their observable fruit by which to decide if or how much I try to fellowship with them or evangelize them.

You will know them by their fruits. (Mt. 7:16, 20; 12:33) Although we, as Christians, cannot claim certain knowledge of others' eternal destiny, we **must** make judgments in order to determine how we are to engage with a given person. Spiritual maturity and wisdom are required to do it well. In the extreme situation of breaking fellowship with someone in the local church, God's word teaches this caution through its precise language. We are told *not to associate with any so-called brother* when he lives in observably contrary ways. We give the benefit of the doubt unless that person gives clear evidence of being lost.

Saved or not saved? I like Solomon's insight: *The end of a matter is better than its beginning.* (Eccl. 7:8) A passed-on saint is a safer bet than an in-process saint. That's because all the evidence has been weighed in, the life has run its course, and all things will be judged righteously. (Eccl. 12:13-14)

And the Apostle Paul concurs: ...*therefore do not go on passing judgment before the time, but wait until the Lord comes....* (1 Cor. 4:1-5)

[If you want more on judging others, see entry #27]

Skewed Ideas Christians Sometimes Hold

#38

When someone says...

I just speak my mind to God—raw, honest, about everything, whatever... even complaining like David did. God can handle it. Jacob wrestled with God!

I apologize, but...

That's not wise.
God is not man.

A few of the enjoiners in Scripture that are often quoted to back up this approach to God are 1 Thess. 5:17, *pray without ceasing* and Phil. 4:6-7, *in everything by prayer and supplication.* David's prayers are certainly earnest and full of emotion, and often cited as an example of freedom of expression to God. Some people like to point back anecdotally to Moses in conversation with God as being *face to face, just as a man speaks to his friend* (Exo. 33:11) as an epitome to which we should aspire.

Those **are** wonderfully rich Scriptures worthy of meditation and putting into practice. However, like **all** passages, they are to be understood within the qualifying whole of Scripture and under divine illumination. So, along with those first two teaching passages from the Apostle Paul to pray about everything all the time, there are also the equally inspired words of

109

I Apologize ...but not like you think

Solomon: *Do not be hasty in word or impulsive in thought to bring up a matter in the presence of God.* (Eccl. 5:1-3) The most heart-wrenching, honest prayers of David were also spiritually informed and displayed a reverence for God. In one of his most complaint-filled Psalms, he catches himself short, realizing, *when my heart was embittered and I was pierced within, then I was senseless and ignorant; I was like a beast before You.* And he tells that he went again into God's presence where he gained a fuller understanding, concluding, *If I had said, "I will speak thus,"* (that is, with the embittered heart) *behold, I would have betrayed the generation of Your children.* (Psa. 73:15, 21-22) In repentance, David's only response to God for the balance of the psalm after that insight was **humble** praise.

Regarding the conversations between God and Moses, the actual wording is that *The Lord used to speak to Moses face to face, just as a man speaks to his friend.* It doesn't say that Moses had that same freedom. God **can** handle it; but can **man**? Moses did dialogue with God, but he learned his comparatively lowly place through many humbling and painful situations, including being barred from entering the promised land of Canaan. *Now the man Moses was very **humble**, more than any man who was on the face of the earth.* (Num. 12:3) And yes, Jacob wrestled with God; but he also got his hip dislocated from its socket. (Gen. 32:24-32) To say the least, He was **humbled**.

So, back to Solomon, and finishing the verse: *Do not be hasty in word or impulsive in thought to bring up a matter in the presence of God. God is in heaven and you are on the earth. Therefore, let your words be few.* (Eccl. 5:2)

I'll say no more.

#39

When someone says...

Information technology advancement, Artificial Intelligence in particular, is inevitable. Christians just need to be aware and careful.

I apologize, but...

The values of IT and AI reflect those of the designers and programmers. The overwhelming majority of leaders worldwide have shown to care little about checked advancement versus monetary and convenience gain. It seems to be only a tiny minority of people who concern themselves with and want to slowly, conscientiously roll out "advancement". Among a plethora of negative consequences, the dehumanizing nature and godless moral vacuum of the general inertia leaves true Christians little hope of freedom, let alone survival. The relatively small percentage of clear-headed Christians in the industry will have little to no overall influence, and in fact, will become the prime target of discrimination. There will be no "safe place" for Christians within the general culture, and especially on the frontiers of AI. Jesus wasn't speaking in hyperbole when he warned His followers, *But be on guard; for they will deliver you to the courts... and you will stand before governors and kings for My sake, as a testimony to them... Brother will betray brother to death, and a father his child; and children will rise up against parents and them put to death.*

***You will be hated by all** because of My name....* (Mk. 13:9-13) Only those believers who recognize their increasingly persecuted plight and prepare at the soul level for it will be able to endure **intact**. Scriptures intimate that many will fall **in line** (both figuratively and literally), receive their "chip" to buy and sell, and lose their Way in the process. *And he causes all, the small and the great, and the rich and the poor, and the free men and the slaves, to be given a mark on their right hand or on their forehead, and he provides that no one will be able to buy or to sell, except the one who has the mark, either the name of the beast or the number of his name.* (Rev. 13:16-17)

Skewed Ideas Christians Sometimes Hold

#40

When someone says...

A Christian should take care of his body as the temple of the Holy Spirit.

I apologize, but...

True. But in order to do that, he has to make sure it's the Temple that he's building up. David wanted to build a temple and was stopped by God. His son, Solomon, was to build it. David's idea was short-sighted, earthbound, temporal. *However, the Most High does not dwell in houses made by human hands; as the prophet says: "Heaven is My throne, and earth is the footstool of My feet; what kind of house will you build for me?" says the Lord, "Or what place is there for My repose? Was it not My hand which made all these things?"* (Acts 7:44-50) As wise and responsible as maintaining a healthy body is, the human "temple" verses (1 Cor. 2:12, 3:16 & 6:19-20) teach different lessons than staying in good physical health. Honoring or glorifying God with our bodies is biblical, but not an excuse to build an earthly temple and sell it as a spiritual act. It's much more about precepts than biceps.

#41

When someone says...

One emphasizes, "Christians shouldn't be lazy." Another says, "Christians shouldn't strive." Which is it?

I apologize, but...

Ecclesiastes 4:4 says it's **both**.

The fool folds his hands and consumes his own flesh. Laziness is not fitting to the believer. *One hand full of rest is better than two fists full of labor and striving after wind.* Striving for sustenance or gain also doesn't reflect Christian calling.

Other Scriptures enjoin us to do both. Proverbs has us learn from the ant to prepare and be industrious. *Go to the ant, O sluggard, observe her ways and be wise. Which, having no chief, officer or ruler, prepares her food in the summer and gathers her provision in the harvest.* (Prov. 6:6-8) There are psalms that praise the value of rest and sleep. *It is vain for you to rise up early, to retire late, to eat the bread of painful labors; for He gives to His beloved even in their sleep.* (Psa. 127:1-2)

Ecclesiastes, as it so often does, puts the complementary truths together. Solomon answers with the call to wisdom, which always looks to God's judgment as the determiner: *There is a time for **every activity** under heaven.* (Eccl. 3:1) Therefore, one appropriate expression of God's way is diligent work. *Sow your seed in the morning and do not be idle in the evening, for you do not know whether morning or evening sowing will succeed, or whether both of them alike will be good.* (Eccl. 11:6) That **is**, give both times a try, **not** the modern inclination and interpretation to work day and night! Another commendable and practical expression is availing oneself of grateful rest from work. *Here is what I have seen to be good and fitting: to eat, drink and enjoy oneself in all one's labor in which he toils under the sun during the few years of his life which God has given him; for this is his reward.* (Eccl. 5:18)

So, which is it? Wrong question. Rather, how do I do both? It requires wisdom from God in the moment. *Rejoice, young man, during your childhood, and let your heart be pleasant during your the days of young manhood. And follow the impulses of your heart and the desires of your eyes* (this is **not** sarcasm). *Yet know that God will bring you to judgment for **all these things**.* (Eccl. 11:9)

Which was laziness or striving and which was commendable effort and rejoicing? The progressive revelation of the New Testament has Paul offering a very direct and pictorial answer to that for us, saying *like a skilled master builder I laid a foundation... but each man must be careful how he builds on it. For no man can lay a foundation other than the one which is laid, which is Christ Jesus. Now if any man builds on the foundation with gold, silver, precious stones, wood, hay, straw, each man's work will become evident; for the day will show it because it is to be revealed with fire, and the fire itself will test the quality of each man's work. If any man's work which he has built on it remains, he will receive a reward. If any man's work is burned up, he will suffer loss; but he himself will be saved, yet so as through fire.* (1 Cor. 3:11-15) In the end, God's testing crucible will reveal what was done in Him (gold, silver, precious stones), and what was not (wood, hay, straw). The man whose life was established on the foundation of Christ lives on, but only some of his actions prove Godward. Even Christians have a little fire to contend with, but it doesn't touch their souls—just their efforts.

What to do, Christian? The Apostle Paul adds God's simple guide: ***Whatever you do***, *do all to the glory of God.* (1 Cor. 10:31)

#42

When someone says...

The Bible is so hard to understand. I can't really quote verses word-for-word and remember exactly where things are in Scripture.

I apologize, but...

Worthwhile things typically are hard.

My guess is that if those making such a complaint or confession were to sit down with me, together we could find several **other** areas in which that person **has** put significant time and effort into knowing numerous facts. It might be songs and lyrics that so easily come to mind... on repeat and won't go away. Maybe names and faces of Hollywood actors or professional sports figures. How about foods one eats, medicines one takes, brands one buys? Almost certainly, there would be mentally-logged facts specific to one's job, memorized policies and laws, necessary codes, practical procedures, etc. The common factor? Those all required repeated exposure and effort over time.

I've heard those same people express how wonderful it would be if Jesus were here in person instead of having just left us His words. His first followers certainly felt that way when He let them know He was leaving. Some even ventured to argue with

Jesus that it couldn't or shouldn't happen. His response? *But I tell you the truth, it is to your **advantage** that I go away; for if I do not go away, the Helper shall not come to you; but if I go, I will send Him to you... I have many more things to say to you, but you cannot bear them now. But when He, the Spirit of truth, comes, He will guide you into all the truth.* (Jn. 16:7-13)

Jesus told us that this *Helper-Spirit of truth* actually authored the Bible and resides inside every believer to help make sense of it. The Bible is not like other books. It's gold, honey, treasure, life. Consequently, it demands digging, tasting, searching...wanting!

And, not all the Bible is hard to grasp or remember. Much isn't. Much of it is simple, practical, understandable. If Jesus or the Apostle Paul showed up in person at many churches today and preached those same words, they would find themselves unwelcome and likely run out with all kinds of scurrilous labels attached. We know that would be the response because the **words** of Jesus and Paul which have been **understandable** for two millennia are today twisted and massaged and rejected in order to fit what people **do** want to hear. Both Jesus and Paul taught clearly about practical matters like finances and stuff, modesty, the poor, marriage, raising children, food, sex, race, gender. And yet, those **understandable** things are the very things progressive Christians in progressive "churches" reject, redefine, and replace with our culture's ideas. In His poignant and beautifully simple manner, Jesus calls them out: *If I told you earthly things and you do not believe, how will you believe if I tell you heavenly things?* (Jn. 3:12)

Think that's unfair to apply to our churches today? Then let me suggest one telling piece of evidence. Most people attending church today can explain psychological terms better than they can theological. They are more conversant concerning obsessive-compulsive disorders, defense mechanisms, passive-aggressive tendencies, and co-dependency than they are concerning sanctification, propitiation, the hypostatic union, and imputed righteousness.

I dare you to take the test!

#43

When someone says...

Have you read so-and-so's Christian book, _____?

I apologize, but...

My typical answer is "No". After 47 years of walking with Christ, I find **nothing** that reads like Scripture. I spend at least an hour each morning meditating on Scripture alone. Weekends and vacations afford even longer sessions. The writings of the earliest "Church fathers", as rich as they are, don't have **that unique mark of inspiration** that Scripture has. I attribute recognizing the difference to one practical habit—I spend the greatest proportion of my spiritual reading and meditation in Scripture alone. That's not a point of hyper-spiritual bragging. Historically, this practice is as plain and common as vanilla. It's a recognition and habit long-known by Christians, but grossly lost by contemporaries, who trade the pure and simple Truth and Source of life for the popularized, psychology-laced, predigested, calculated, cranked-out superficial. Christian bookstores are stuffed with it and are nearly as off-putting as and more cringe-worthy than Spencer's gift stores!

The well-worn pulpit illustration of bankers recognizing a counterfeit dollar bill by constantly gazing on **the real thing** is profoundly apropos. Contemporaries just don't know it or believe it. They think the digested works of mere men can better and more efficiently synthesize and pass along the knowledge of God. They are tragically misguided. The result leaves them spiritually stunted. They have no idea how different an experience it is to nod in agreement with the insight of a human author than to revel in astonishment at the perfectly crafted and personally delivered Word of God itself!

The law of the Lord is perfect, restoring the soul;
The testimony of the Lord is sure, making wise the simple.
The precepts of the Lord are right, rejoicing the heart;
The commandment of the Lord is pure, enlightening the eyes.
The fear of the Lord is clean, enduring forever;
The judgments of the Lord are true; they are righteous altogether.
They are more desirable than gold, yes, than much fine gold;
Sweeter also than honey and the drippings of the honeycomb.
(Psa. 19:7-10)

Once again, Solomon had surpassing insight: *The writing of many books is endless, and excessive devotion to them is wearying....* (Eccl. 12:12)

Including this one.

#44

When someone says...

Christians should be positive people, not negative people. Positivity is Christian.

I apologize, but...

Today's popular concept of positivity is a false notion, and the imposing of it on Christianity is a colossal category mistake. Christianity does not teach positivity. Christianity **teaches truth, reality**. The highly prevalent notion of the power of positivity is merely a man-centered manipulative shtick that large sectors of the Church, sadly, have built upon; in fact, whole denominations, theologies, and bookstores-full are based on its false narrative (most charismatic doctrines employ it as foundational; the likes of Joel Osteen epitomize those deceived and deceiving).

Despite the scads of books and sermons touting it, no verse in the Bible has God calling Christians to be positive people. He calls them to be many things that **are** positive, but that is a very different thing. To conflate the two shows a misunderstanding of the basic Christian message, the Gospel itself. **Many** verses are ripped out of their sockets and twisted to humanistic positivity. A few Scriptures popularly misused that way are Phil. 4:13, Eph. 5:20, Gal. 5:22, Jas. 1:2, and Mt. 6:33. One passage that might look most like a contender for this notion is Phil.

*4:8-9—Finally, brothers and sisters, whatever is true, whatever is honorable, whatever is right, whatever is pure, whatever is lovely, whatever is commendable, if there is any excellence and if anything worthy of praise, **think about these things**. As for the things you have learned and received and heard and seen in me, **practice these things**, and the God of peace will be with you.* No doubt, these are positive things to meditate on and practice. However, it is **not** the thinking on them or even the practice of them that **makes** them positive. The list of words starts with **true**, and all are referring to God-designed and infused realities, not man-derived or imbued notions. If one can't see the difference in the two, he or she doesn't understand the very difference between Christianity and humanism! That's the point here.

Romans 8:28 is also a beloved "go to" as power for positive thinking. *And we know that God causes all things to work together for good to those who love God, to those who are called according to His purpose.* Salesmen of positivity blindly make a few blatant errors (or lies) in using this passage. They omit the actual parts about God and redefine "good." They basically gut the verse and start over. Rightly read, God is both the Source (*God causes*) and Goal (*love God*) in this reality. Good is not earthy or man-perceived positive outcomes, but rather eternal Kingdom outcomes that, I might add, **often** come in the earth-bound form of tragedies, pain, suffering, sacrifice, humiliation, poverty, deformity, marginalization, victimization, death.

Truth as taught in Scripture also includes huge negative realities such as: all men are desperately selfish at their core; this world will hate Christians and not appreciate them; God will destroy this earth because of its sinful brokenness; the huge majority of human beings will reject God and experience the eternal suffering of separation from Him, all He is and offers. These negatives transformed into goodness by God in His Kingdom ways are a far cry from the earthly nice outcomes of health, wealth, prosperity, and the notion that man is basically good, which the purveyors of positivity in churches have sold us.

No, Christians are **not** called to be positive. They are called to be loved by God and to be faithful to Him. I'm positive of that.

#45

When someone says...

Christians have 2nd Amendment rights also. And it makes sense for a church to protect its families with armed security or congregants "packing".

I apologize, but...

Where do I begin? The first most glaring inconsistency is the confusion of Church and State. Where **is** your citizenship? *Our citizenship is in heaven....* (Phil. 3:20) That's not a platitude, but a declaration of fact for the Christian. Although the Church is subject to civil laws, its allegiance and directives come from a totally different and higher Source, which will at times unequivocally counter civil rights and defy civil laws. In a sense, we have dual citizenship while we're still on this terrestrial ball, so we do our best to navigate this world with these words of Jesus in mind: *Then render unto Caesar the things that are Caesar's, and to God the things that are God's.* (Lk. 20:19-26) But when God's design conflicts with our national "rights", we unhesitatingly relinquish the latter. Peter and the other apostles, when under attack, rightly embraced their heavenly citizenship priority: *We must obey God rather than men.* (Acts 5:29) When red, white, and blue clash with heaven's crystal clarity, Old Glory bows and heavenly glory reigns supreme!

I Apologize ...but not like you think

Second, the most basic and profound teachings of Jesus' beatitudes include turning the other cheek and giving away more than your pursuer asks. In short, we don't live in this world with the same self-concerned and self-defending priority that non-Christians often have. It's actually true, Christian, that *Our help is in the name of the Lord, Who made heaven and earth.* (Psa. 124:8)

Third, the Christian must remember that *though we walk in the flesh, we do not wage battle according to the flesh, for the weapons of our warfare are not flesh, but divinely powerful for the destruction of...arguments and all arrogance raised against the knowledge of God.* (2 Cor. 10:3-5) The world's obsession with self-preservation through one-upping force is understandable because that's all they know and have. The one who claims Christ, but prefers to arm himself with the world's means, reveals his actual basis of trust.

Christian, have you not learned from Jesus' clear rebuke of Peter to put down his literal sword (Mt. 26:51-56; today's equivalent – carrying permits?) and to take up the sword of faith? Don't you remember that it was the falsely religious Jews who had a temple guard with a captain (Acts 4:1-12; today's equivalent - armed church security guards?) who were called upon to put Jesus' apostles in jail? And why? Because Peter and John pointed out how messed-up their supposed faith was—*Jesus Christ... whom you crucified.*

Christian, drop your guns and pick up your Sword of the Spirit!

#46

When someone says...

Our pets are part of the family. They'll be in heaven, won't they? What about the lion lying down with the lamb verse?

I apologize, but...

Christians, of all people, should be those least concerned about these types of questions (little children's innocent and naive curiosity aside). It reveals a distraction from the core concern of God's revelation and a deplorable sense of proportions. Americans as a society have lost sight of the nature of things, but Christians should not follow along. Americans currently devote something on the order of $260 billion annually toward their pets. All the while, over 3.4 billion of the worlds' human population lives on less that $6 a day. That same pet money redirected could change that suffering one third of the world's human income to $6.21 a day. It's not the solution to their poverty, but it illustrates the impact of the choices we make. There are any number of ways to demonstrate a potential reallocation of funds, but the bottom line is this: Americans demonstrate by their practical, bottom-line habits that they know and care more about Buffy, Blacky, and Bandit than they do about Ahmet, Akemi, and Alejandra.

Speaking of God's creation priorities, James 1:18 says *In the exercise of His will He brought us forth by the word of truth, so that we would be **a kind of first fruits among His creatures**.* Man in God's image is unique, and animals are not first or even equal. Animals are a beautiful part of God's creation and are to be treated with **appropriately weighed** respect. One could possibly ponder unclear biblical "what if's" about pets having souls, pets in heaven... or alien life on other planets. However, to wander into mysteries "out there" while tripping over revelation "right here" is profound foolishness and great tragedy. Packed passages like 1 Cor. 15:42-58 and Mt. 25:31-46 say **nothing** about animals, but **much** about humans and their eternal destinies. The famous pastor and theologian, Harry Ironside, apparently answered the "pet" question graciously by inferring that if the person reached heaven and needed their pet there to be happy, it would be there. His generous answer left unsaid how unlikely it would be that one seeing the lovingkindness of God face-to-face might still want Buffy!

Finally, don't fall for the rationalization that there's no reason why we can't embrace both (a popular American justification for our luxuries), when the hard facts and numbers show that we **don't**! We adjust life around and pamper pets while we ignore humans unnecessarily suffering and dying. Once again, it's understandable when non-enlightened people live such, but when Christians do the same, it's collectively unconscionable.

Maybe it's time to let some of our pet projects die.

#47

When someone says...

Christians have complete freedom to pursue any career, barring outright sinful activity.

I apologize, but...

Let me offer two alterations or qualifications to that sentiment:
* Christians' foundational freedom is rescue **from** sin and **to** righteousness. (Rom. 6:18)
* Just because something is permissible, it isn't necessarily fruitful or God honoring. (1 Cor. 6:12)

Start at the right reference point. Concerning work or career choice, rather than start with man's freedom, start with God's supremacy in all things. Instead of entertaining an endless list of potential jobs to be considered, start by asking God to allow you to work in an arena of greatest glory to and fruit for Him given how He's designed you and where He's placed you. That starting point of reference established, now venture into evaluating specific career roles. Being an accountant or investment broker may not be outright sin (although I would argue it's the very rare person who escapes a career focused on money without being deceived to some degree), but is it the wisest stewardship of life for those few souls plucked from the world's craving masses (I'm referring to the minority of Christians in the world here.)? That's a better question with a significant and different priority. I would argue that there are plenty of world-lings willing and desirous to shuffle and count others' money. Certainly there are millions of other job options. How likely is it that programming computer games, designing high-fashion clothes, doing stand-up comedy, or becoming a bodybuilder is God's plan in sanctifying you and serving mankind?

Most explanations I hear by Christians defending worldly or frivolous career paths follow some version of three easily devised paths:

1) **the straw man path of extremes** ("Are you saying that it's sin to work with or make lots of money?") – a most insincere approach to conversation or pursuing God's will
2) **the pragmatic path** ("We still have to live in the world and make a living.") – a tipping-of-the-cards revealing that the person's bottom line is still the bottom line
3) **the spiritualized path** ("If Christians don't enter and influence that field, then the world will take it over.") – a naive attempt to gloss earthbound concern with heavenly smoke

These explanations ignore the God-priority that has supposedly reversed one's entire direction for living, and rush to defend what one is really concerned about and still wants at this point. The world.

SECTION H:

SEEING BUT NOT BELIEVING

#48

When someone says...

How do you explain so-called "evil people" and those of other religions thriving or living to old age?

I apologize, but...

There is an answer. *In the generations gone by He permitted all the nations to go their own ways; and yet He did not leave Himself without a witness, in that He did good and gave you rains from heaven and fruitful seasons, satisfying your hearts with food and gladness.* (Acts 14:16-17) *He causes His sun to rise on the evil and the good, and sends rain on the righteous and the unrighteous.* (Mt. 5:45) That only says something about the character of God (His immense love and patience), not mankind's character. Put bluntly, He's better than you and I are.

You might ask, "So then, He treats those who accept Him and those who reject Him the same?" There is an answer. Those verses only speak to His patient and generous ways during man's **earthly** life. It's not the end of the story. After the sun, rain, fruitful seasons, food, and gladness, He generously warns us all that *it is appointed for men to die once, and after this comes judgment.* (Heb. 9:27) The judgment will reveal two different responses by humans. The humble, wise man thanks his Creator and Sustainer, knows he is an unworthy receiver

Seeing But Not Believing

of goodness, and says, *But God will redeem my soul from the power of the netherworld, for He will receive me.* The proud and foolish *when he dies he will carry nothing away; his glory will not descend after him. Though while he lives he congratulates himself... he shall go to the generation of his fathers; they will never see the light. Man in his pomp, yet without understanding, is like the beasts that perish.* (Psa. 49) As Paul Harvey used to say, "Now you know... the rest of the story."

#49

When someone says...

This world is insane!

I apologize, but...

Yes, it literally is. You're agreeing with Scripture with that assessment. *I directed my mind to know, to investigate and to seek wisdom and an explanation, and to know the evil of folly and the foolishness of madness. This is an evil in all that is done under the sun, that there is one fate for all men. Furthermore, the hearts of the sons of men are full of evil and insanity is in their hearts throughout their lives. Afterwards they go to the dead.* (Eccl. 7:25; 9:3)

But realize this, that in the last days difficult times will come. For men will be lovers of self, lovers of money, boastful, arrogant, revilers, disobedient to parents, ungrateful, unholy, unloving, irreconcilable, malicious gossips, without self-control, brutal, haters of good, treacherous, reckless, conceited, lovers of pleasure rather than lovers of God, holding to a form of godliness, although they have denied its power; Avoid such men as these. (2 Tim. 3:1-5)

But a natural man does not accept the things of the Spirit of God, for they are foolishness to him; and he cannot understand them, because they are spiritually appraised. (1 Cor. 2:14)

For even though they knew God, they did not honor Him as God or give thanks, but they became futile in their speculations, and their foolish heart was darkened. Professing to be wise, they became fools. (Rom. 1:21-22)

Put up against its all-wise, all-knowing, and all-benevolent Creator... yes, the world is insane.
Or was your exclamation just a momentary outcry of frustration, but not really meant as an accurate assessment of this world? Think again....

There is no such thing as an abstract morality. (in <u>Of Human Bondage</u> by William Sommerset Maugham)

#50

When someone says...

Most people need therapy at some time. Modern culture creates so much stress.

I apologize, but...

Modern culture has certainly compounded stress and multiplied opportunities to embrace it willingly; but stress has always been present and has but one effective, broad-spectrum cure—*the peace of God.*

The **key** is not comprehension of the observable causes. Modern psychology, which rules the day, offers incredible insight into the multi-layered, practical, superficial causes and manifestations of anxiety, depression, breaks with reality, etc. But it stops there. Our therapy culture offers no cures and little help in arresting the inexhaustive problems. Psychologists and therapists are like bird watchers who can identify all manner of species by subtleties of color, size, flight, and calls... but have no idea how to repair one, let alone create one.

Only in The Truth are found the means of addressing the root problems (*all have sinned and fall short of the glory of God* - Rom. 3:23) and the ultimate goal being sought (*the peace of God which surpasses all comprehension* - Phil. 4:6-7). Modern psychologists reject the root death-cause in every one of us,

Seeing But Not Believing

and God as the singular and unique life-Source. So therapists offer endless trial-and-error experiments to those souls who trust them instead of trusting their Maker Who alone heals the soul.

#51

When someone says...

What's with this current generation of young people? They're so messed up and lost.

I apologize, but...

For what it's worth, it's not a figment of your imagination. The concerns are real and profound. At its roots, this generation is **innately** no different than any other. Man's nature is basically unchanged over the millennia. However, this generation has inherited not only history's ever-compounding factors, but a unique warp-speed coefficient that radically multiplies the total outcome.

What's in common? Youth have always been the product of culture, parenting, and plain old youthfulness.

What's unique? Modernity's universal media communication with its inevitable by-product of virtual "reality" has reached a point of overtaking the capacities of young people to handle it. Let me try to synthesize the resulting current generation in four descriptives (culturally sensitive compulsory caveat—I'm generalizing; this doesn't necessarily apply to your little Johnny or Mary, of course).

PROPORTIONS: This generation has lost a sense of proportions. Especially due to the glut of information, today's young people are without discernment between what is of import and what is trivia, what is true and what is false, what is real and what is fantasy. And even more alarming, they often lack the conviction that those differences exist! Much of the constantly available input they devour is superfluous, carnal, or outright wicked. Not only are they not led to see and delineate proportions, but they now lack the ability intellectually and morally to do so. They react as strongly to a fast-food order wrongly fulfilled as to the broadcast of the latest school mass shooting. "Awesome!" describes both a storm over the Grand Canyon and the latest TikTok shuffle. The findings of a highly accomplished research scientist on a given topic carries no more weight than a fifteen-year-old YouTube influencer's snarky post on the same topic. Image over content is the norm. I can't improve on Dennis Miller's succinct eloquence - "Never have lives less lived been more chronicled." If nothing else, the fact that today's ridiculous advertising actually works evidences that post-modern humans cannot discern fact and fiction, truth and lies, important and trivial, good and bad.

PROGRESSIVENESS: Today's "progressive" culture thinks they are automatically advanced simply because they've **seen** things. I've heard a young person claim to be one with and love the outdoors and nature, while rarely leaving her room and computer screen. She loves only the **idea** of it, but really thinks she loves it. Similarly, it's been asserted that the casual use of vulgar language, including the F-bomb, is progress because "it doesn't mean anything, it's just an expression." That doesn't impress me as growth or making headway. "Progressive" is today's deluded misappropriation for actual regression or deterioration.

SELF-CENTEREDNESS: The emerging generation takes self-everything to a new level. They have been ingrained with the belief that they are the center of their own existence. No matter what you attach to it, one finds self at the center of this generation's concern, resource, valuations, and goal. Self-indulgence (old-fashioned carnality), self-sufficiency (delusion), self-reflection (navel-gazing), self-validation (circular logic), self-focus (I-dolatry). Psychology has become their uncontested religion with themselves receiving all offerings of worship!

PRESUMPTION: Today's young person often embodies the irreconcilable marriage of despair and cock-eyed optimism. They desperately flail about in depression because every pursuit manifests an inevitable down side, disappointment, failure to deliver. (It's not called "the fall" without reason.) In the same moment, they naively embrace the "hope" that it will all turn out okay if they look within, which is the exact opposite place they need to search. Their youthful passion for "fun" never grows up to sensible responsibility mixed with appropriate, actual joy. Combining the two derailed, diametrically opposed attributes, they live out a conflicted mess of meaningless wishfulness.

Yes, people are people, all innately made of the same stuff and potentials. But not all generations of history are the same. This one is bearing the weight of all the previous ones converging at a unique point of genuine crisis… which will prove true what Christians have more than just plastered on T-shirts, billboards and placards at sporting events, but uniquely known all along to be core reality:

For God so loved the world, that He gave His only Son, that whoever believes in Him shall not perish, but have eternal

Seeing But Not Believing

life. [but there's more...] *For God did not send the Son into the world to judge the world, but that the world might be saved through Him. He who believes in Him is not judged; he who does not believe has been judged already, because he has not believed in the name of the only begotten Son of God. This is the judgment, that the Light has come into the world, and men loved the darkness rather than the Light, for their deeds were evil. For everyone who does evil hates the Light, and does not come to the Light for fear that his deeds will be exposed. But he who practices the truth comes to the Light, so that his deeds may be made manifested as having been wrought in God.* (John 3:16-21)

SECTION I:

EXCUSES FOR NOT BELIEVING

I Apologize ...but not like you think

#52

When someone says...

I'm not antagonistic toward Christianity. I just don't see the evidence.

I apologize, but...

Question One: In honesty, how much have you earnestly searched it out to have determined that the evidence is not there? The word "evidence" implies research or study. I would simply point out that the entirety, every detail, of the created universe points clearly to its Creator.

Question Two: How much researched evidence do you have that points to an alternate viable conviction about the source and meaning of everything? God anticipated and corrects man's false claim of "not enough evidence" by saying, *For the wrath of God is revealed from heaven against all ungodliness and unrighteousness of men who suppress the truth in unrighteousness, because **that which is known about God is evident within them; for God made it evident to them**. For since the creation of the world His invisible attributes, His eternal power and divine nature, **have been clearly seen, being understood through what has been made**, so that they are without excuse. For even though they knew God, they did not honor Him as God or give thanks, but they became futile in their speculations, and their foolish heart was darkened.* (Rom. 1)

146

Excuses For Not Believing

Personally, I don't see the evidence for my iPhone's amazing displays and sounds being produced by invisible signals sent from one place on our globe to a satellite in space and then to my phone. It's not because the evidence isn't there; it's just that I haven't seriously looked into it enough to discern and appreciate its genius. And yet, despite my not knowing the details, there's one thing about my phone that I don't doubt at all. I am absolutely convinced real, intelligent beings made my phone. It's not the making of my own fantasy or something that spontaneously generated. That would be absurd.

#53

When someone says...

The church is full of hypocrites. I'm not a Christian because of all the hypocrites.

I apologize, but...

Sadly, the first claim exaggerates on a semi-valid charge. *Because the sentence against an evil deed is not executed quickly, therefore the hearts of the sons of men among them are given fully to do evil.* (Eccl. 8:10-11) These verses observe evil men being religious all the way to the grave! When the Church compromises with individuals, they eventually adjust God's ways and morals allowing systemic failings and sin to become the norm. Those "churches" often justify the confrontation of **none** as being a loving form of fellowship and the invitation of all (seeker friendly services) as a loving form of outreach. In actuality, by doing so, they've become the world with religious trimmings. Thus, the reason Jesus Himself was much more harsh with hypocrisy than with non-believers' garden variety sin.

And still... to levy "hypocrites" as the reason for one's unbelief is more akin to scapegoating or gaslighting—choosing to discount or ignore the real ones because of fakes. It's hiding behind hypocrites. Something has to be smaller than an object to hide behind it. Are you **not** an athlete, musician, student,

Excuses For Not Believing

employee, parent, etc. because of all the rotten ones of those you've observed? (That was hopefully rhetorical.) Then, no, that's **not** why you're not a Christian. You've possibly not come to know real Christians up close. If you had, you'd see Christ in them; and in seeing Him, you'd be tempted to become a real one yourself!

#54

When someone says...

He's so heavenly minded he's of no earthly good.

I apologize, but...

It's possible. However, the more typical scenario is that people are so earthly minded that they're of no heavenly good. God showed both to Solomon: *Do not be excessively righteous and do not be overly wise. Why should you ruin yourself? Do not be excessively wicked and do not be a fool. Why should you die before your time?* (Eccl. 7:17)

Some possible examples of being *excessively righteous and overly wise*:
- * counting every calorie and working out no matter what
- * guarding against all unnatural products or rejecting modern scientific progression
- * never jay-walking or letting your speedometer go 1 mph over the limit
- * reading "all the best books" on a topic
- * never missing Mass or being in church every time the doors are open

Some possible examples of being *excessively wicked and a fool* (all counterpoints to the examples above):
- * eating, drinking, and leisure with abandon

Excuses For Not Believing

* believing everything that claims science as its source or embracing technology indiscriminately
* increasingly testing your limits with speed, heights, thrills
* accepting mainstream and social media as your source of information
* claiming agnosticism or atheism without earnest searching

Both extremes can kill the body and soul. And quite apart from their divergent approaches, either pursuant might get run over by a rogue truck!

So, what to do? *It is good that you grasp the one thing and also not let go of the other; for the one who fears God comes forth with **both** of them.* (Eccl. 7:18)

Some possible examples of *grasp and also not let go*:
* eating and exercising sensibly... and splurge on a special occasion
* realizing you can own a new generation computer and not take it with you camping
* obeying the road laws, but letting your parking meter run out for a good cause
* read broadly, selectively, thoughtfully... and ditch most media
* searching for God with all your heart, soul, mind, and strength... and see if He doesn't find you!

This kind of balance or tension is extremely hard, equally rare, and incomparably worthwhile.

#55

When someone says...

What kind of god allows evil and then would kill his own son to fix the mess?

I apologize, but...

I know that everything God does will remain forever; there is nothing to add to it and there is nothing to take from it. (Eccl. 3:14) God being eternal and perfect can only enact what is of those two qualities. He cannot improve on it. But what of the fall? Yes, even making man with the potential to choose and fail had the stamp of eternality and perfection. God didn't change course. His plan to address the fall intrinsically and appropriately included **re**demption, **re**conciliation, **re**storation, **re**newal, **re**creation, **re**turning things to what they were eternally and perfectly meant to be. And what of the seemingly unthinkable and unjust sacrifice of His Son to accomplish it? *Greater love has no one than this, that one lay down his life for his friends.* (Jn. 15:13) Take it literally. The perfectly unified Trinity of Father, Son and Holy Spirit tells us that there could be no greater enactment or display of love than for Them to self-sacrifice for us. They agreed as One to rescue us—broken, rebellious creatures—and embrace us as friends. ***No greater love* was possible!** To have **not** included it in their plan would have been less than eternal and perfect. You cannot improve on perfection. [Some of you may remember Fonzie & the mirror scene?]

Excuses For Not Believing

And can it be that I should gain
an interest in the Savior's blood?
Died He for me who caused His pain?
For me, who Him to death pursued?
He left His Father's throne above,
so free, so infinite His grace!
Emptied Himself of all but love,
and bled for Adam's helpless race!
Amazing love, how can it be
that Thou, my God, shouldst die for me?
[**And Can It Be?** – Charles Wesley]

All glory to **that kind** of God - eternal, perfect, incomparable love incarnate!

#56

When someone says...

I've met lots of religious people and they sure haven't made me want to be one of them.

I apologize, but...

I'm with you! Similarly, fast food gives me indigestion and makes people unattractive lumps. The problem is one of mistaken identity. Religionists and Christians aren't the same thing. Religion and Christianity aren't the same thing.

Religion is the invention of man to find, reach, please, or appease his conception of god or gods. The one true God reveals Himself to His created people without those manmade requirements or intentions. Those who understand and follow His call have no need for those unattractive religious ways. They follow and worship Him in fitting and beautiful ways. They are rightly called His disciples, His worshipping followers.

Jesus pronounced, *All authority has been given to Me in heaven and on earth. Go therefore and make disciples of all nations, baptizing them in the name of the Father and the Son and the Holy Spirit, teaching them to observe all that I have commanded you; and lo, I am with you always, even to the end of the age.* (Mt. 28:19-20) Jesus called for followers who recognize Him as Lord and emulate His teachings, not religionists who invent spiritual recipes for the Church to follow. The Apostle Paul wrote, *The things which you have heard from me in the presence of many witnesses, entrust these to faithful men who will be able to teach others also.* (2 Tim. 2:2) The Apostle Paul called for followers who would faithfully pass on the message and teaching of Jesus, not the religious practices Paul had left behind once coming to right belief.

But... most of mankind resist God's simple offer and revert to a host of religious notions which I agree, are unattractive, in addition to empty-ended. To go back to my opening analogy, religious people are like fast food eaters. When they're hungry, they find tantalizing offerings everywhere, along every highway, cheap, easy, quick. Jesus didn't even imply that he wanted religious followers or gatherings (churches) that are a common, greasy place offering something partly real food and mostly tasty filler that looks appealing on a billboard, stimulates many to take the off-ramp, pull out some small change, swap it for a paper bag at the drive-through, and shovel it down while on the road to where they really think they want to get. In wild contrast, He called us to join Him for a banquet, at a secret, cozy cafe hidden far off the beaten path, where real food is slowly, skillfully prepared, offering nutritious delights that demand all the money in our wallet, a lifetime of hours, personal interaction with our Chef, convinced that it **is** the place to which we really wanted to get!

Jesus called for disciples, not religious people. Jesus promises complete fulfillment and therefore requires complete commitment. It isn't even close to the quick, easy, air-brushed thing advertised as golden arches that leaves one with an eternal gut-ache. Why do so many people choose to go back for more fast food religion? Because it's easy, cheap, and gives a brief pleasure that **simulates** real taste and health, but isn't. They don't know any better, don't believe the real thing is that much better, don't think it's worth the investment of time and money, and don't want to believe what they've previously tasted is killing them.

Religious people attract masses for a quick bite prepped by a minimum-wager right off the expressway. True Christians invite others to join their Master Chef for a secret banquet far off the road paved with good intentions.

Enter by the narrow gate; for the gate is wide and the way is broad that leads to destruction, and there are many who enter through it. For the gate is small and the way is narrow that leads to life, and there are few who find it. (Mt. 7:13-14)

#57

When someone says...

Christianity is a bunch of "Thou Shalt Nots". What's the appeal of avoiding all the fun and exciting things in this life? And a god who demands that to let you into heaven? No thanks!

I apologize, but...

I'm so sorry you've heard or thought that. It's not that way at all!

The efficacious giving up stuff and suffering of Christianity has been already done and finished; and not by Christians, but *for* them by Christ. For starters, Jesus voluntarily left His rightful Prince's position in heaven's perfection in order to come live and die with us and like us here. (Phil. 2:6-8) For finishers, He voluntarily paid for all mankind's sins by humiliatingly taking on and **becoming** all mankind's sin on a torture tree. (Heb. 12:2; 2 Cor. 5:21)

Christians don't give up good things or take on tough things in order to earn heaven. That work has all been done once for all by Christ. (1 Pet. 3:18) Unlike the ascetic Hindu, they don't deprive or hurt themselves in order to please God. Such self-made religion accomplishes nothing eternally. (Isa. 44:9-20; 1 Cor. 13:3) When Christians who understand the Gospel give something up, it's more like C. S. Lewis pictured it—like little children who give up playing in mud puddles for the opportunity of having a holiday at the beach!

Don't get me wrong. We followers of Jesus **do** voluntarily give up things (little "crosses") in order to *share the sufferings of Christ* and *know...the fellowship of His sufferings*—sometimes even our most prized relationships and our physical lives. (Mk. 10:28-30) But, we're not doing it because it lessens the burden Jesus carried. He still took on **all** the work of salvation to rescue us from spiritual death. We do it out of thankfulness, wanting to be with and like One Who would do such a thing for us! And on top of all that... there will be an unending holiday at the beach.

Come join us... *Thou shalt!*

SECTION J:

AND ONE TO GROW ON

I Apologize ...but not like you think

∞

When someone says...

Who needs religion? What's the big deal? I can find my own way or make my own path.

I apologize, but...

It's the biggest deal there is. You can try to make your own way, but you better know **all** there is to be known in the universe if you plan to design the path through it. That age-old approach doesn't seem to be working very well in terms of preventing humans from cheating, lies, theft, rape, murder, war, prejudice, anxiety, insanity, sickness, and... that "little" thing that awaits us all—death. The thing that started all that mess is recorded in this ancient spirit-human interaction:

*Now the serpent was more crafty than any beast of the field which the LORD God had made. And he said to the woman, "Indeed, **has God said,** 'You shall not eat from **any tree** of the garden'?" The woman said to the serpent, "From the fruit of the trees of the garden we may eat; but from the fruit of the tree which is in the middle of the garden, God has said, 'You shall not eat from it or touch it, or you will die.'" The serpent said to the woman, "**You surely will not die!** For God knows that in the day you eat from it your eyes will be opened, and **you will be like God, knowing good and evil.**" When the woman saw that the tree was good for food, and that it was a delight to the* *eyes, and that the tree was desirable to make one wise, she took from its fruit and ate; and she gave also to her husband with her, and he ate. Then **the eyes of both of them were opened, and they knew** that they were naked; and they sewed fig leaves together and made themselves loin coverings.* (Genesis 3:1-7)

The serpent, Satan, displayed a few of his most despicable inventions:
    Casting Doubt – ***Has God said?***
    Twisting Words – ***Any tree?***
    Schmoozing – ***You surely will not die!***
    Embedding Evil into Good – ***you will be like God, knowing good and evil***

The diabolical schemes worked and the first two humans swallowed the lie that they could be the gods of their destinies. But no sooner had they taken that first bite than they were enlightened… to see what a horrible decision it was! *Then **the eyes of both of them were opened, and they knew** that they were naked.* Being **physically naked** wasn't the problem. It was realizing they weren't God, but had tried to be! They were **spiritually naked**. That's what gave them the shivers. And ever since then, mankind has been sewing fig leaves trying to hide and cover-up.

"Fig leaves" come in all colors, shapes, and sizes these days – religions and philosophies, politics and laws, psychology and TED Talks, Hollywood themes and icons, sporting heroics and heroes, disorders and therapies, diets and reconstructive surgeries, investments and get-rich-quick schemes, pornography and morning-after pills, Oscars and Got Talent shows, guy gadgets and gal fashions. And we're still shivering and looking for loin cloths.

We have devised some paths but, if we're honest, they aren't working. Despite modernity's "advancements", we find ourselves wandering naked in a desert still looking for the latest off-ramp to somewhere better, somewhere safe, somewhere meaningful and rewarding. I hate to sound like a broken record... I apologize, but... the real God alone has the solution.

A voice is calling, "Clear the way for the Lord in the wilderness; make smooth in the desert a highway for our God." (Isa. 40:3) He **is** coming back. Now is the opportunity to get on the right path.

Therefore, strengthen the hands that are weak and the knees that are feeble, and make straight paths for your feet, so that the limb which is lame may not be put out of joint, but rather be healed. (Heb. 12:12-13) You and I need to simply recognize our limp, and cooperate with God's cure.

"Behold, I will do something new, now it will spring forth; will you not be aware of it? I will even make a roadway in the wilderness, rivers in the desert." (Isa. 43:19) God alone is and can do it. What an offer!

This book is not the way. These short entries are only warning signposts, pointing to the Way. *He is the Way and the Truth and the Life.* (Jn. 14:6)

AFTERWORD

Once to Every Man and Nation
James Russell Lowell
(1819 – 1891)

Once to every man and nation,
Comes the moment to decide,
In the strife of truth with falsehood,
For the good or evil side;
Some great cause, some great decision,
Offering each the bloom or blight,
And the choice goes by forever,
'Twixt that darkness and that light.

Then to side with truth is noble,
When we share her wretched crust,
Ere her cause bring fame and profit,
And 'tis prosperous to be just;
Then it is the brave man chooses
While the coward stands aside,
Till the multitude make virtue
Of the faith they had denied.

By the light of burning martyrs,
Christ, Thy bleeding feet we track,
Toiling up new Calvaries ever
With the cross that turns not back;
New occasions teach new duties,
Time makes ancient good uncouth,
They must upward still and onward,
Who would keep abreast of truth.

Though the cause of evil prosper,
Yet 'tis truth alone is strong;
Though her portion be the scaffold,
And upon the throne be wrong;
Yet that scaffold sways the future,
And behind the dim unknown,
Standeth God within the shadow,
Keeping watch above His own.

He said, "Go, and tell this people:

'Keep on listening, but do not understand;
And keep on looking, but do not gain knowledge.'
Make the hearts of this people insensitive,
Their ears dull,
And their eyes blind,
So that they will not see with their eyes,
Hear with their ears,
Understand with their hearts,
And return and be healed."

Then I said, "Lord, how long?" And He answered,

"Until cities are devastated and without inhabitant,
Houses are without people
And the land is utterly desolate,
The Lord has completely removed people,
And there are many forsaken places in the midst of the
land."

Isaiah 6:9-12

ABOUT THE AUTHOR

Family
Born to family—common, white collar, small town, conservative, semi-religious, mid-west, secure home, steady Dad, gregarious Mom, older brother, younger sister, "perfect" middle child; married & madly in love 41 years, 3 incredible daughters with good men, 12 amazing & entertaining grandchildren, we'll see...

Education
Ohio public school, BA in Business, Bowling Green State University; ThM in World Missions, Dallas Theological Seminary; Post Graduate in Brick Wall Method

Places & Languages
Raised in Ohio, lived in 8 states and 3 cities of Turkey, lengthy sojourns in Guatemala and Greece, traveled in 45 states & 12 countries, mentally wandering the globe; fluent in English, comfortably speak Turkish, stumble around in Spanish, read Greek, and fake it in Hebrew

Work
Lawn mowing, lifeguard, hay bailer, farm market clerk, painter, electrician's lackey, carpenter, insurance agent, swimming pool cleaner, custodian & groundskeeper, youth pastor, stone mason's assistant, missionary, mining company sales rep, college career counselor, pastor, roofer, carpenter, pastor, office cleaner, handyman, pastor, NFL player's estate manager, worldwide servant, construction company gallimaufry man, tired, hopeful of being retired

Play
Youth AAU swimming, football, basketball, water skiing, track & field; college pole vaulting & decathlon; French horn, guitar, drawing, singing; landscaping; rock climbing, lifting, tennis, running, hiking, walking, slowing

Stuff
Music eclectic & moving, handy-craft hack, reading & writing, lover of beauty in all its forms

Essence
Christian, remarkably forgiven, discipleship, exhorter, teacher, inexplicably blessed, Christian

JIM'S MEMOIR

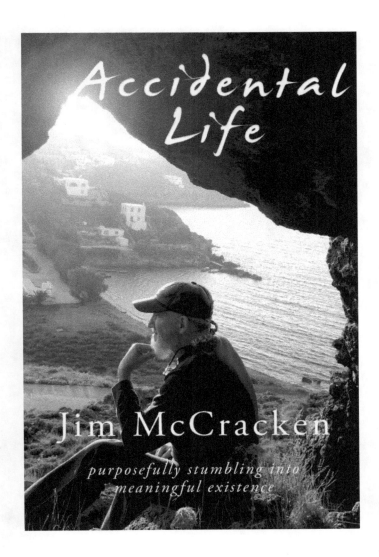

Printed in the USA
CPSIA information can be obtained
at www.ICGtesting.com
LVHW091100290524
781182LV00008B/779